Kakuma Girls

Sharing Stories of Hardship and Hope from Kakuma Refugee Camp

Clare Morneau and contributors

BARLOW BOOKS
fine books for enterprising authors

Library and Archives Canada Cataloguing in Publication data available upon request.

ISBN 978-1-988025-14-8 (paperback)

Printed in Canada

To order in Canada:
Georgetown Publications
34 Armstrong Avenue
Georgetown, ON
L7G 4R9 Canada

Principal Photography by Jjumba Martin
Cover, inside cover, pp 6, 8, 12–13, 24–25, 29, 32, 35, 36, 39, 40, 43, 45, 47, 50, 55, 60, 63, 64-5, 66, 72, 79, 81, 82–83, 92–93, 95 (middle & bottom), 97, 99, 101 (bottom), 102–103, 108–9, 126–127, 131, 132, 134, 139 (top), 141 (top), 142, 144, 148, 152–153, 164–165, 182–183, back cover

Clare Morneau pp 17, 133, 168–169

Carol Devine pp 75, 95 (top), 101 (top & middle), 104, 128, 136, 139 (bottom)

Kakuma Girls: pp 19, 31, 69, 130, 135 (top), 137, 146, 150. Images courtesy of Harriet, Rita, Ifere, Fardosa, Saharo, Koshe, Nura, Rothrossy, Brenda, Sylvia, Irene, Terry, Christine, Cecelia, Aluk

pp 20 UNHCR/C. Wachiaya

pp 68 Brendan Bannon/IOM/UNHCR

pp 122 Courtesy of Niki Sennik

pp 157 Storey Wilkins

pp 158 UNHCR/Wendy Stone

Havergal College pp 129, 131, 141 (bottom), 143, 145, Susan Pink, pp 135 Lois Rowe

Edited by Carol Devine
Designed by Isabel Foo
Produced by Doug Laxdal, The Gas Company Inc.

For more information, visit **www.barlowbooks.com**

Barlow Book Publishing Inc.
96 Elm Avenue
Toronto, ON
M4W 1P2 Canada

Contents

Foreword

The one thing that refugees have in common is the fear of not being heard. Clare and her classmates have made such a great impact by choosing to communicate with girls whose world they can only imagine. When I was a young girl living in a refugee camp there weren't a lot of possibilities or even dreams for my future. At times I felt an immense sense of isolation as our lives were always in the midst of change due to ongoing war.

Friendship has been a way without boundaries to connect with others. The friendships I made in Africa are still intact as we have shared experiences and stories. A connection is often what makes the difference in someone's life. I am proud of what Clare and her classmates have done to make a positive impact and reach out to girls in the Kakuma refugee camp.

Educating girls is a relatively new venture in Africa. Now that more and more countries are seeing the importance of educating girls, the narrative is changing. But there are still a lot of obstacles. Culturally, girls are expected to marry at a young age and that leads to the risk of leaving school, or becoming a mother at such a young age without proper education on reproductive health. The more girls are educated the more their communities will thrive.

Reading each of the girls' stories I am transported back in time to a place where my spirit and body stand still. But in every essence and in spite of their realities the girls have so much hope. I share a personal connection with all of the girls. I see myself in each and every single one of them in terms of their yearning for education, family responsibility, and unwavering talent. I have fallen in love with their ambition and eagerness to have a better future. The young women's futures are so limitless because of the education they are getting. As I have learned, the past shapes the future and your story becomes your strength.

The girls' stories moved me and I am so pleased to have had the privilege to hear them. The girls are examples of the hope that the future holds for the continent of Africa and our fight for gender equality. Their strength, courage, self-esteem, dignity, willingness to adapt and spirit will make them an asset to their communities. Thank you to all who have contributed. This book is both educational and emotive.

Kuoth Wiel
Actress, Model and Humanitarian,
Refugee from South Sudan,
based in Los Angeles, CA

Preface
An Oasis, a Sisterhood

Morneau Shepell Secondary School for Girls (MSSSG) is like an oasis to the girls; it is a safe haven, an invaluable gift. It is a place that provides them safety, comfort, and most importantly, time. Time to focus on what matters most—their academics. Refugee girls face a myriad of challenges in the camp, such as early marriage and sexual and gender-based violence. This affects their participation and enrolment in school as they enrol at an advanced age and drop out early. MSSSG is a multicultural community of like-minded girls who come from over ten countries and have different backgrounds but are brought together by their desire to become great individuals. These girls have a golden opportunity to focus on their education, a luxury they could not afford if they were learning in other schools. The burden of taking care of the family and doing household chores has been lifted from their shoulders so they can focus on their futures. They learn from each other and build each other up, and all this is possible because of the stability that MSSSG provides.

The girls' communication with the Havergal students has developed into a beautiful relationship. Most of these girls have no worldview or perspective beyond the camp. As such, their communication with the Havergal girls has opened up their minds to endless ideas, dreams, and possibilities. They have learned so much about their school, their culture, and how they deal with everyday life. They see themselves in each other and even though they may be miles apart and culturally diverse, they feel as close as sisters. This connection has given the MSSSG girls hope for their future, and they are working hard toward realising their dreams.

Mohamud Hure
UNHCR Education Officer, Kakuma

Catherine Wachiaya
Public Information Associate,
UNHCR Sub-Office, Kakuma

Africa

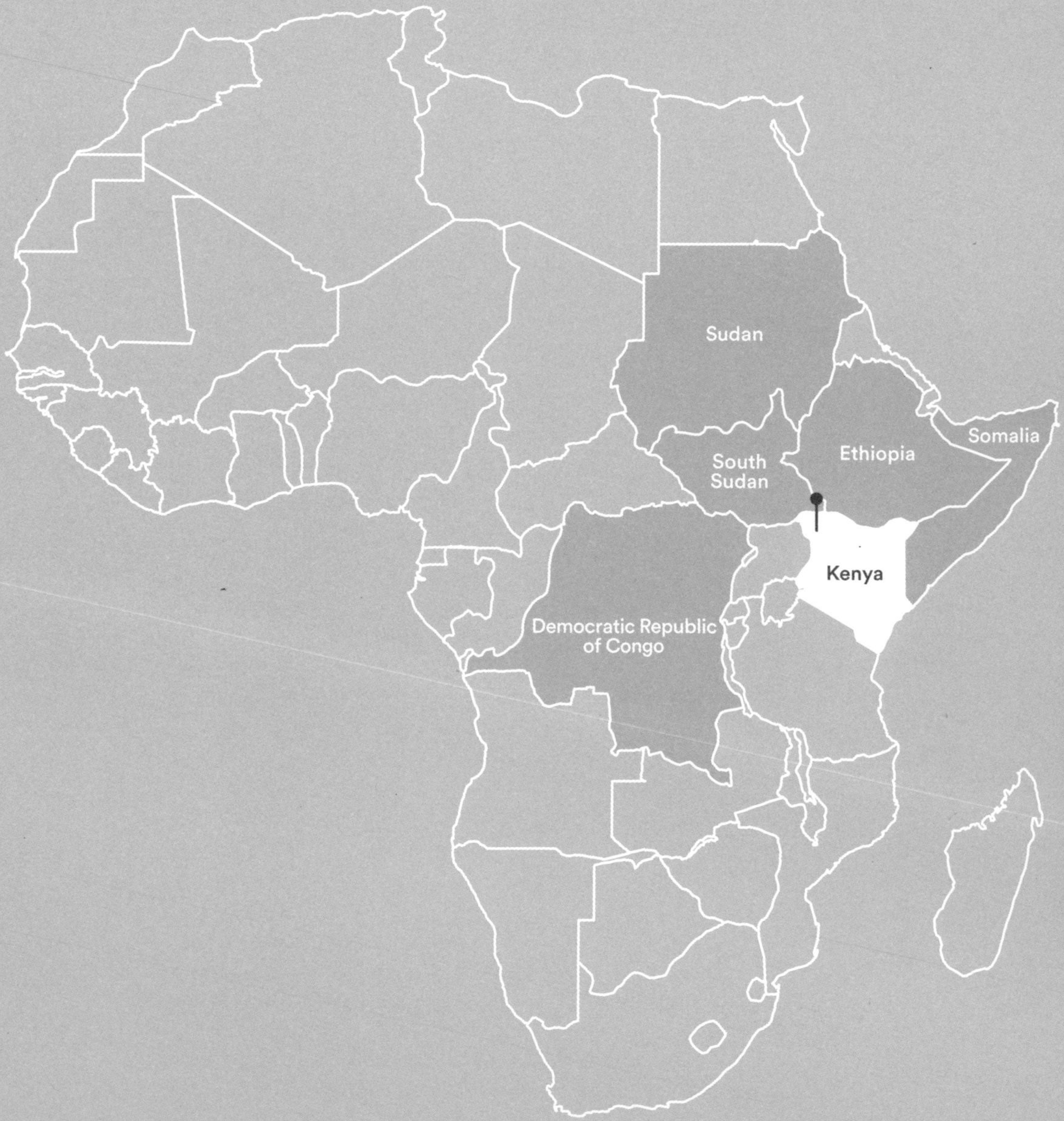

Sudan

South
Sudan

Ethiopia

Somalia

Democratic Republic
of Congo

Kenya

Kenya

Kakuma
○

Turkana County

Rift Valley

Eastern

North Eastern

Dadaab
○

Nyanza

Central

Nairobi
●

Coast

Introduction

Discovering Kakuma

I'm Clare and I'm 17 years old. I'm in grade 11. I live in Toronto with my parents, three siblings and my dog.

I want to tell you about a girls' school in a refugee camp in Kenya called Kakuma. I also want to tell you about friendships between teenage girls at my school and girls in Kakuma.

I first heard about Kakuma Refugee Camp when my dad and the company he worked for, Morneau Shepell, visited the camp. About four years ago, with the help of my uncle who works for the United Nations High Commissioner for Refugees (UNHCR), my dad and some employees from Morneau Shepell along with Panther Kuol, a former refugee who lived in Kakuma, got involved with the camp. They decided to build a technology centre there. At that time refugee issues began to come up during our family dinners.

I already knew I was lucky to live in Canada because I'd learned a lot from my sister Grace, who is from Uganda. I was also starting to learn about the situations, good and bad, in other countries in Africa. Before this exposure I often ignored the violence and fear in the world. I did not know about the destructive dictators, brutal civil wars, corruption, and famine that tormented some countries in Africa and around the world. Millions of people have been forced to flee their homes and I had no idea this was happening. I also didn't know a lot about the rich history, culture and diversity of the African continent.

When my dad and colleagues were in Kakuma, they saw the real need for girls' education. They visited the schools in the camp and talked to members of the UNHCR and other aid organizations about what was needed there most.

And that was girls' education. So they decided it was something the company wanted to support. The UNHCR agreed it would be valuable to create a dedicated girls' secondary school given the challenges girls face in obtaining education in Kakuma. Morneau Shepell supported the building of the school in 2013. It opened in January 2014.

Morneau Shepell Secondary School for Girls (MSSSG) is a fundamental part of over 300 girls' lives in Kakuma. Currently only two per cent of eligible refugee children go to secondary school in Kakuma and a minority of those are girls. This is a shocking percentage, one that seems almost impossible to someone living in a first-world country.

The main idea of MSSSG is to enroll studious, hardworking girls while also helping the most vulnerable girls in the camp. Girls who are orphaned or only have one parent, or those who lack family support and protection, are at a disadvantage. They have no means of earning money and they risk being pulled from school to care for siblings, do tasks such as collect firewood, or get married. If they go to MSSSG they can stay in school, be safe, and focus on their education.

My dad and I started to discuss the school often. I was lucky to see photographs of the students. These girls intrigued me; I wanted to know where they were from and how they'd arrived at the school.

I go to Havergal College in Toronto. Havergal is an all-girls, private day school, but students can also board, so there are some international students. Havergal has about 900 students. It's a really great school and students there are well supported.

Not long ago I knew nothing about refugee camps or Kakuma and many of my friends at Havergal didn't either. I decided that I wanted to change this.

By exploring the Kakuma girls' world, I had a chance to explore my own. I was getting a perspective that is rare for a typical Toronto private school student, and I wanted my friends and classmates to have this opportunity, too.

I realized we had to get in touch. I wanted to do something more personal than be an invisible donor. If we did a book or other kind of fundraising drive I wanted the girls in Kakuma to say, "This is a book from a girl I know at a secondary school in Toronto. This is from one of my friends."

Writing letters, penpal-style, seemed the best way to get started.

I've always loved writing letters. I lived in France for a year when I was eleven, and while I was there I would write letters to my friends all the time. It was awesome getting a letter back, something handwritten, I loved looking at my friends' handwriting, the photos they sent, and the little decorations on the letters.

So I started a partnership in which Havergal girls signed up to write letters to girls at the school. In Kenya, Mohamud Hure, an Education Officer for the UNHCR, found interested girls at MSSSG. Mohamud put the girls into penpal pairs. Thirty girls signed up for the partnership on each side, making sixty participants in total.

At Havergal we have something called the Institute or the Forum for Change. The teachers at the Forum encourage students to pursue ideas we have for making change. Through this Forum I told girls about the opportunity to join a letter-writing partnership with Kakuma girls. I haven't relied on Havergal for the partnership, but I book meeting rooms at school and I share news about the partnership with the Forum for Change and various Havergal news outlets.

I thought that, through writing letters, we Havergal students could expand our worlds by learning about refugees. Sometimes we were pushed to go to school when we didn't feel like it, when girls in Kakuma would give everything to experience the opportunities and education we are lucky enough to receive.

I decided that the partnership should be centred on education. We could share a window into our world, one where getting a secondary and university education is expected.

I thought that the girls at Morneau Shepell in Kakuma needed to know that Canada is a safe place to live, a country where educating girls is, for the most part, as important as educating boys. I also knew that the girls in Kakuma had something that many Toronto girls did not— a true appreciation and appetite for education, one that cannot be stopped by conflict or literal hunger. Torontonians value education, but many have grown accustomed to it being a right, not a privilege. I thought we girls could be peer supporters and mentors for one another.

So we began. Some Havergal girls typed their letters and I printed them out to send. Other girls handwrote and decorated them. I gathered the first letters from the Havergal girls and sent them to Kakuma Refugee Camp.

My dad brought home a folder from work with letters he'd received from Morneau Shepell in Kakuma. "They're here!" I said to myself. I couldn't believe it—it was the coolest thing to hold those girls' letters in my hand. It felt like Christmas morning. The Kakuma girls' letters were handwritten because they don't have computers at their school.

The first letter I read was from a girl named Rita. I'm amazed by her. Rita came alone to Kakuma from South Sudan. She returned to South Sudan to reunite with her family after many years. Not only had she managed to live without them, but when they asked her to stay with them, she said no and decided to travel back to Kakuma. She knew she wouldn't get an education in South Sudan. It's incredible that Rita put her education first. I couldn't wait to share the letters with the girls at Havergal.

This first exchange of letters was soon followed by Skype calls, which were exciting for us on both sides of the globe. The Internet connection was poor in Kenya and the voices of the girls faded in and out, but we got to see each other's faces and the girls got to talk to their writing partners. The conversations were group calls with a bunch of us in Toronto and a bunch of girls in Kenya. These calls were priceless, even if on some days they only lasted a few minutes.

We found so many similarities between us and the girls at MSSSG. We talked about our favourite classes and sports; we talked about the future. During Skype calls sometimes the girls in Kenya had power outages, and once some of the Havergal girls couldn't make it to the call because of a snowstorm.

After a Skype call, the Havergal girls would say many things to me. "They're so sweet." "I love being in touch." "We're more alike than I thought: We have Facebook and the same favourite subjects in school." "They're just like us. Except they are not. One girl's mom died after she was shot in a war."

It's important to say, while we may be the same, our circumstances are not. It's clear that girls in Toronto have many more opportunities for education and wellbeing, and to us, survival is far less of a concern than it is to a refugee girl. We have access to scholarships, community colleges, and other resources that allow us to believe that there will always be a way, whereas in Kakuma, university is *the* dream.

We had quickly learned so much about each other. I wanted something material from the exchange that we could hold up for ourselves and others to see.

Something to hold in your hand

Through this correspondence, I got the idea for this book. I want the voices of the Kakuma girls to be heard, and I want to show how education fosters hope.

I think the book is a way to get more people involved in refugee issues. This year has seen the largest refugee movement ever in history. If this book helps people understand that, while we may have music, career aspirations and role models in common with refugee girls, they have experienced so many more challenges than most people living in North America and other first-world countries, then it's worthwhile.

For those who already know about refugee issues or were refugees themselves, I hope they see something familiar in the dignity, struggles, and strength of these girls and they learn something new about Kakuma Refugee Camp.

I hope girls in Canada and elsewhere will read the stories from Kakuma, be moved, and have the opportunity to get involved in refugee issues. I want to personalize these girls' stories so the bigger issues are less scary to face and address.

I loved the film *The Good Lie*. It's a true story about Lost Boys and a Lost Girl from South Sudan who fled to Kakuma and then had the chance to resettle in the US. I like the honest way it tells the story of refugees' lives and the violence of war they experienced. The movie has Hollywood sparkle, but it goes deeper than that as three actors were former refugees and two were also Lost Boys, unaccompanied children who fled from South Sudan. It makes refugees and their stories less intimidating. You see the unbelievable journey of these individuals and you feel you are there with them. And you care about them.

My hope is that readers will feel similarly immersed in the stories of the Kakuma girls. We're still getting to know one another, but already we want to tell you some stories. The girls at Morneau Shepell Secondary School for Girls are not the "other"—we are equals. We have different lives, geography, and social conditions, but we are all young women living in this world today with hopes, fears, and dreams.

The Need for Girls' Education

History of the Morneau Shepell Secondary School for Girls

In 2008, Morneau Shepell, Canada's largest human resources services firm, began looking for a way to make a difference in the world, wanting to give back and do more than just donate money to a charity.

The idea of helping refugees came from a desire to do something that was not at all related to the company—a desire to reach outside of their community and create an impact somewhere else in the world. Morneau Shepell made a goal to start a project that their diverse employee body could rally around.

After consulting with the UNHCR, the firm decided to help the Kakuma Refugee Camp because of the need for education for refugees who often spend years—or even lifetimes—in Kakuma. Morneau Shepell started by building a technology centre in the camp so refugees could learn about modern technology and build skills that would help them if they had the chance to move elsewhere. The technology centre was opened in 2012 and now offers classes many times a day. Hundreds of refugees have received diplomas from this training centre.

The idea to build a school for girls came from a trip to Kakuma Refugee Camp in November 2010. Bill Morneau, the company's chairman at the time, and several other staff members were opening the technology centre. They took a tour of the camp and visited its schools, where they noticed a lack of resources and trained teachers. Children often sat on rocks or behind crowded desks, and classes sometimes consisted of hundreds of students and one teacher. Most importantly, they were shown graphs that indicated that boys and girls attend school in equal numbers at the age of eight, but by thirteen and fourteen, few girls are still

enrolled. Many girls stay home because it is not safe for them to walk the long distances to day schools, while others do because their parents would rather spend money sending their sons to school. Girls are also typically expected to do the housework, and are sometimes married off at a young age.

After this visit, the idea to build a boarding school for girls was born. This model would ensure that girls would not have to place themselves in dangerous situations by walking to school, or risk being pulled from school by families who couldn't afford uniforms or books. This school was founded with the intention to give girls in Kakuma Refugee Camp a chance to get ahead.

Havergal College

Havergal College is an all-girls school located in Toronto, Canada, for girls from Junior

Kindergarten to grade 12. The school was established in 1894 and was named after Frances Ridley Havergal (1836–1879). She was a poet as well as a writer of hymns and children's books. Just over 900 girls currently attend Havergal College, including around fifty student boarders. These boarders represent a diverse array of countries, including China, Mexico, and the United States, and bring many new cultures to the Havergal community.

In 2006, the school established the Forum for Change, a department specifically dedicated to helping students develop their original ideas about how to get involved in their community and the world. It is an essential part of Havergal where new ideas are valued and explored.

The Forum has fostered the Kakuma Toronto Girls Education Partnership. It has been a place to discuss new ideas and approaches, and a home for our early morning Skype calls.

History of Kakuma Refugee Camp

In the 1990s, Sudan's civil war caused many adolescents to flee the country and seek asylum. These children, known as the Lost Boys of Sudan, first arrived in Ethiopia, where they established a children's encampment with the help of aid organizations like the United Nations High Commissioner for Refugees (UNHCR). In 1991, this encampment was destroyed and many of the Sudanese had to return to Sudan or travel to Kenya.

In 1992, the UNHCR and the Kenyan government created Kakuma Refugee Camp. The camp was initially established to accommodate 23,000 Sudanese refugees. Nowadays, it accommodates refugees from countries all over sub-Saharan Africa, including Somalia, Ethiopia, and the Democratic Republic of the Congo.

Initially, many Sudanese were displaced by a civil war that lasted from 1983 to 2005. As their villages were destroyed, numerous Sudanese people were forced to trek to Ethiopia, where they resided until their refugee camp was attacked. These Sudanese then crossed back into Sudan in order to get to Kakuma Refugee Camp in Kenya. Even after the civil war, the outpouring of refugees from South Sudan (independent since 2011) and Sudan continues, with many civilians fleeing a political power struggle and persecution based on ethnic grounds.

Many refugees also travel to Kakuma from Somalia. In the 1990s, after the collapse of Siyad Barre's dictatorship in Somalia, civilians who had received weaponry from Barre began to fight back against militias. Many villagers fled Somalia in order to avoid getting caught in the crossfire.

Ethiopians make up a smaller portion of refugees residing in Kakuma. Many Ethiopians fled to Kenya in the 1990s after the government was overthrown and new policies were created that caused an ethnic divide in the country.

Over the years, the population of Kakuma Refugee Camp has fluctuated. Overall, it's gone up to far over capacity. In 2011, the camp experienced a major decrease in population, as many South Sudanese were able to return to South Sudan after the country gained independence. However, when fighting in South Sudan began again in 2013, these South Sudanese fled back to the camp and the camp's population began growing rapidly again. There are currently over 181,000 refugees living in Kakuma, with this figure increasing daily.

Kakuma Refugee Camp

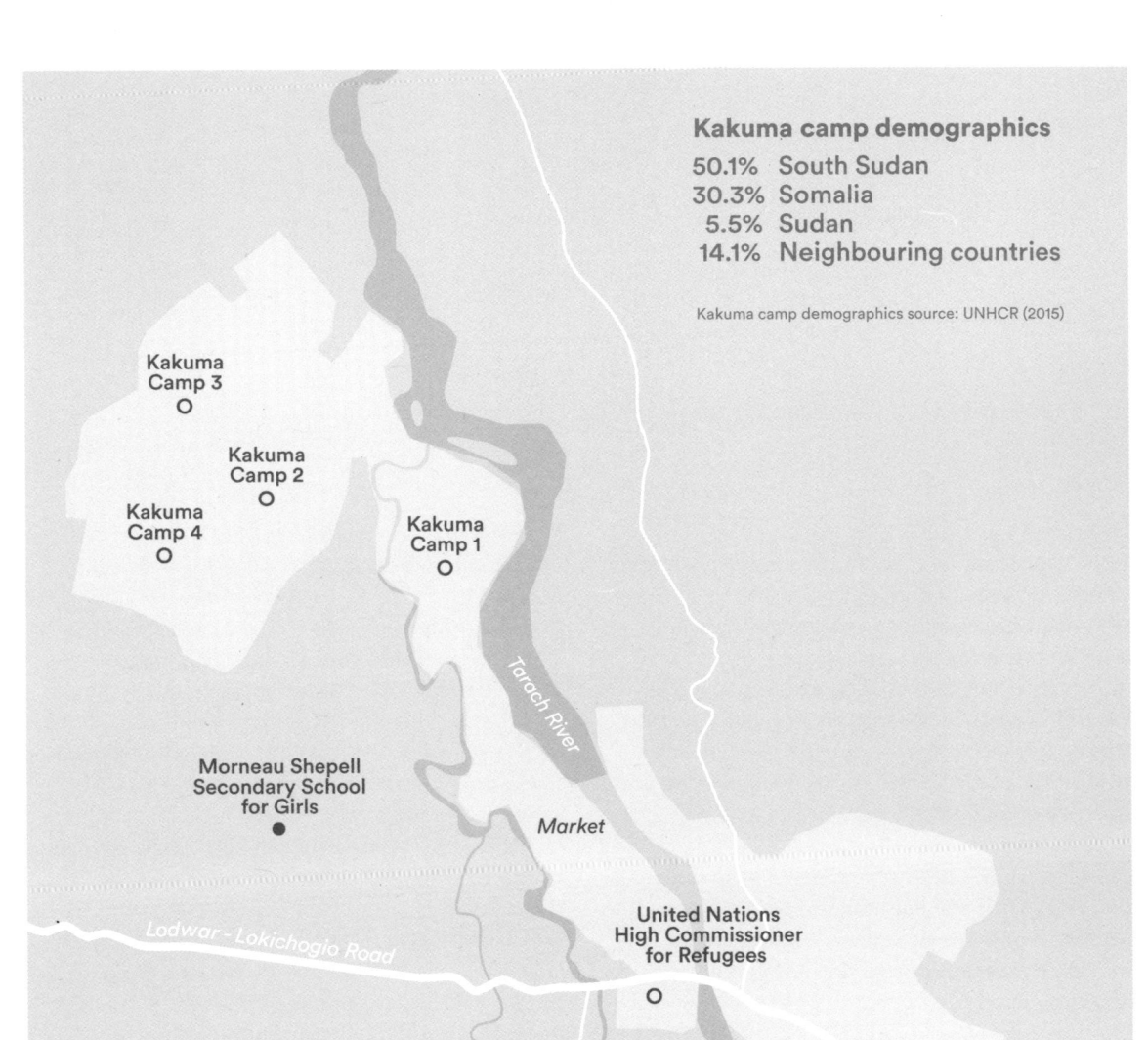

Kakuma camp demographics

50.1% South Sudan
30.3% Somalia
 5.5% Sudan
14.1% Neighbouring countries

Kakuma camp demographics source: UNHCR (2015)

Kakuma
Camp 3

Kakuma
Camp 2

Kakuma
Camp 4

Kakuma
Camp 1

Tarach River

Morneau Shepell
Secondary School
for Girls

Market

Lodwar - Lokichogio Road

United Nations
High Commissioner
for Refugees

At the moment, it is only possible for Kakuma to help refugees because of the support it receives from humanitarian organizations and the Kenyan government. Although there are many agencies involved in the camp, it is difficult for them to maintain the standard of aid that is needed for the refugees, including for education, shelter, and water. Aid organizations often struggle with budget cuts and have problems helping the sheer number of refugees in need.

The UNHCR is responsible for the camp overall and works with partners in the UN, as well as in intergovernmental and nonprofit organizations. For example, The World Food Programme (WFP) supplies most of the food to the camp, the Lutheran World Federation helps run the Reception Centre, and the Kenya Red Cross helps with tracing and family reunification in the camp.

The UNHCR

The United Nations High Commissioner for Refugees, better known as the UNHCR, was created in 1950 by the United Nations General Assembly. This branch of the United Nations was established in order to focus on refugees and their rights. It strives to ensure that all refugees are able to find asylum in another country if they do not feel safe in their country of origin, with an option to return home voluntarily, integrate locally, or resettle in a third country.

The UNHCR provides assistance to refugees and internally displaced people by supplying them with the basic goods they need in order to survive. With partners, the UNHCR seeks to minimize the environmental impact of refugee operations.

Since its creation, the UNHCR has helped millions of people around the world. Not only does it create shelters like refugee camps in order to help those who are fleeing violence, it also has a mandate to help stateless people.

The UNHCR depends on all countries to treat refugees and displaced people humanely. It depends on them to respect rules and regulations surrounding the rights of refugees, such as their right to flee and seek asylum. But many countries breach the legal framework.

It is the UNHCR in Kenya that oversees education in Kakuma Refugee Camp alongside implementing partners.

Kakuma Girls Speak

South Sudan

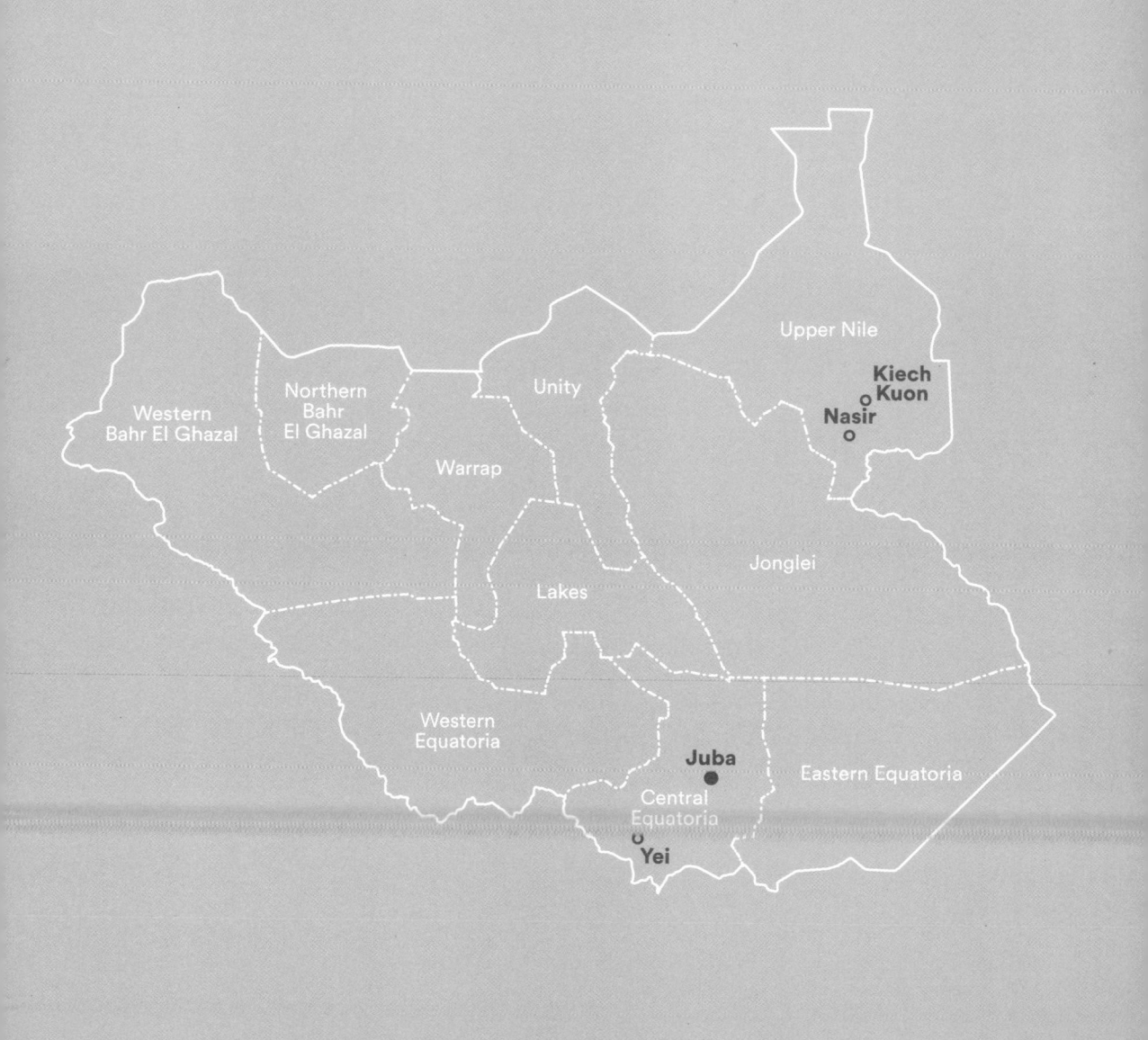

Western
Bahr El Ghazal

Northern
Bahr
El Ghazal

Unity

Upper Nile

**Kiech
Kuon**

Nasir

Warrap

Lakes

Jonglei

Western
Equatoria

Juba

Juba

Central
Equatoria

Yei

Eastern Equatoria

Rita Monday Tom

I was born in Cewale Village. My birth took place at home because in those days there were no hospitals due to my country being underdeveloped. Both my parents were present during my birth.

My name is Rita Monday Tom. My lovely mother gave birth to me when both my grand-parents had passed on. I am the fifth-born child in my family. Otherwise, I have four sisters and four brothers. The firstborn is Buri (thirty years old), the second is Poni (twenty-seven), the third is Jandi (twenty), and the fourth one is Kenyi. After me, the sixth is Dwoki (seventeen) and the seventh is Ladu (twelve). Our youngest is Nyambur (six). All our names are traditional.

"When I arrived to the camp, I felt happy because of the security in the camp. I wished that my parents were here with me."

My family is a polygamous one. I have aunts, uncles, and cousins back in the village. Religion is important in my life because God has pro-tected me ever since I was born. I am a Christian by faith. We practice our religion by singing songs, dancing and worshipping on Sundays.

I am from the recently independent country, South Sudan. My country is not a peaceful country because the leaders are corrupt. There is gunfire every day.

I was separated from my parents when war broke out in 2005. I had to run for my dear life. I didn't know actually where I would end. The trip was not good. It was tiresome and troublesome.

I didn't know where I was to go because in those days there were poor means of transport and communication. We met with many boys and girls during our travelling. We didn't know any other language apart from our mother tongue. We parted ways and everyone went in his or her own direction for safety.

My arrival to Kakuma was not easy. I got sick on the way. The vehicles we were using were lorries and they made lots of noise, but by the will and grace of God I reached safety.

When I arrived to the camp, I felt happy because of the security in the camp. I wished that my parents were here with me.

Since I arrived at this camp, I have never visited any place apart from Kakuma. My house is made of mud. My new home is not a city nor a town. Kakuma is like a village. The camp is comprised of people of many nationalities.

I attended classes one to four at Unity primary, then studied at Angelina Jolie Primary School, which was then the only girls school in the camp. I completed my class eight and I passed very well at the Kenya National Examination Council. I was happy for that and proceeded ahead.

In Angelina Jolie I wore a uniform. It was free since I could not afford one. We had textbooks but there were not enough for the pupils in the school. I have never had a chance to use a computer in my life. We are really eager to use computers in secondary schools for better understanding of the subjects. The main challenge facing me is that sometimes during holidays, I am interested in studying, but I don't have the right books because of lack of finances and that affects me very much.

Actually I don't know what to study in university, but I am hoping to study medicine. When I grow older and have a family, I think I should go to my homeland and live there because east or west home is the best. I am hoping that if I look back at my life if God wishes, I will have lived happily with my children and a good family, and I will have an enjoyable future and a bright one.

I am in grade ten this year. I like the grade because when I complete grade twelve I will have achieved what I have always night-dreamed of. That will be the greatest accomplishment of my life.

Everything is simple. With a personal commitment you will see yourself making every step forward. I have a friend who always encourages me in everything I do at home and at school. She is my best friend because when I need hope she always gives me encouragement.

I have lived in Kakuma for ten years. There are many other people from my home but we are not related to them. Life is not that good since I depend on WFP and UNHCR for everything. These are organizations that provide for refugees, including our education. I concentrate on this education so I can have a better future and provide for myself.

Days in school are good, but sometimes I feel bored, especially on Saturdays. The teachers are giving us their best. My best days in the camp are school days and my worst are vacation days because of the hard life in the camp. Sometimes I go hungry for three days without eating anything. When I get some food, I give it to my younger brothers. Truly life is all about struggle.

The schools in the camp are good and the teachers are really trying their best. I got to Morneau Shepell Secondary School because I performed well during my Kenya Certificate. The teachers are good and encourage us to be role models in future life. I live 15 km away from my school.

We do not choose subjects until we get to form three. Nevertheless, I like the science subjects because I have a dream to become a doctor, if God wishes. I am going on well with the classes and struggling for my life because education is about committing yourself to better the future.

I do not know how or where my family is because I am in Kakuma as a refugee with my younger brothers. My parents live in Southern Sudan. I went to Southern Sudan in 2013 to get them when the war broke out again. I met my family after an eight-year separation. In 2006 we were separated, and in 2013 I went back to Sudan to see my family.

My family asked, "How did you live in that place [Kakuma]?"

They said to me, "Don't go back there. Stay."

But I said, "Education is important."

So I came back to Kakuma because of the war.

Clare: Rita's story is a prime example of how education can profoundly affect refugee girls. She is grateful for the opportunity to go to school and realizes that without the education she has received, she could already be a young mother. She is incredibly determined and will not let any obstacles prevent her from building the life she wants, even if she has to sacrifice things and people close to her to go to school.

When news reached Kakuma Refugee Camp that South Sudan had gained its independence from Sudan in 2011, South Sudanese refugees travelled back home in droves, excited to have a chance at a real life. The population of Kakuma Refugee Camp decreased dramatically, dipping down to 80,000 refugees for a brief few months. Rita travelled back to South Sudan in 2013, miraculously finding her family after being away for so long. However, the peace in South Sudan was short-lived, and war broke out again. Rita was separated again from her parents and most of her family.

Many South Sudanese have travelled back and forth to South Sudan as a result of the frequent stops and starts of the conflict there,

and have lost any sense of hope. Imagine finally believing that you are safe and are living in your own country, and then having that torn away from you yet again. This cycle of despair and hope is well known to many South Sudanese people.

Arriving in Kakuma Refugee Camp is a relief for many refugees. They finally feel safe from the persecution and danger they have fled, and are hopeful that they will receive better treatment in Kakuma. Refugees are greeted in the reception centre and are provided with basic supplies by the UNHCR and other aid organizations. For many, arriving in Kakuma is a bittersweet experience. They have fled from danger and have finally reached asylum. But the camp is not easy to live in. Many refugees struggle with food shortages and the paralyzing sense of dependency they feel when relying on humanitarian organizations for provisions. They are not allowed to work outside the camp. Many refugees like Rita, whose parents are not in the camp, are forced to depend entirely on the UNHCR and WFP as they have no other sources of income or support.

Nhial Alek Tabitha

Life in my country is not easy to cope with because every day there is war, and you cannot sleep a single minute without hearing gunshots.

My name is Nhial Alek Tabitha and I was born in Southern Sudan in a village called Magali on May 15, 1997. I was born at home because there was no hospital near our home.

There was a woman who helped my mother deliver me, but none of my grandparents was present. I have two brothers and two sisters, Achol (sixteen), Choi (twelve), Rech (eight), and Akima (two).

Both my parents love me and my siblings. My family is polygamous, but my father could not feed all of us. I've heard about my stepfamily but I have never met them.

Religion is important in my life because it helps me to promote national unity. I go to church on Sunday and practice singing as a choir member, reading the Bible, and visiting the needy.

I am from Southern Sudan and life in my country is not easy to cope with because every day there is war, and you cannot sleep a single minute without hearing gunshots and knowing people are being killed.

My family and I came to Kakuma to look for peace and to live in harmony. My former home was destroyed during the war and we had nowhere to live. When we were coming to Kakuma I was still young and I could not even tell how the trip was. I had not attended school back in my country.

"I have never used a computer because it is not easy to come across one, but I wish to have one."

My life in Kakuma is very hard because I am staying with my sisters and brothers and I struggle to support them. I would love to see them continue with their education. Neither of my parents are with us due to many problems at home.

I have lived in Kakuma most of my life, and the surroundings are good because all my neighbours are friendly and socialize with us.

I have attended school in Kakuma throughout my life. I started my preschool in Surati, where life was very hard. Then I went to Fuji Primary School. The schools in the camp are not good. We wish that the UNHCR would build other schools, because the classrooms are not big enough and the students have to sit on stones.

I have never used a computer because it is not easy to come across one, but I wish to have one. School is ten kilometres from my home. My favourite subjects are English and Physics. The best thing when living in the camp would be to pass very well and go to a good university, and the worst would be to fail and continue struggling with life.

I passed well in my exams, so I now go to Morneau Shepell Secondary School. I like it so much and the classes are not difficult. My best friend is called Angeth Atem Gak. She is a very humble, honest, respectful, and disciplined girl. The teachers usually support us both to reach our goals.

I want to become a journalist or engineer. I look upon Julie Gichuru, a Kenyan journalist, as a role model. I want to go to university to further my studies, and I wish to study mechanical engineering there.

When I grow older I wish to live in my country so as to build it and help the needy and support the poor. I would like to have children of my own to care for and love. I hope to have a good life in the future, and to donate some of my property to the poor to improve their lives.

What really affects me most is the sickness of my mother and the condition my family is in. During holidays, I do not get to study because I do not have textbooks to read at home. I really feel sad because we are staying at home alone without any parental guidance.

Clare: Nhial is a strong and determined young woman. She knows what she wants and is willing to fight for it. It's hard to believe that she and her siblings are not living with their parents.

Julie Gichuru, who Nhial cited as her role model, is not only a successful Kenyan TV presenter and criminal lawyer but also one of the most influential women in the country. She is a brand ambassador for several humanitarian organizations and an inspiration for many refugee girls in Kenya. Gichuru did not come from a wealthy family. She shows girls that if you work hard at your education, anything is possible. As a female role model, she shows refugee girls that women can be or do anything and be successful.

Nhial also wants to take part in the rebuilding of South Sudan. She knows what is needed in her country and aspires to contribute. South Sudan is in desperate need of proper infrastructure. At the moment, approximately 93 per cent of private homes in South Sudan are made of grass or mud. South Sudan has never had solid, reliable buildings, but some buildings that were once considered sturdy have been compromised by war.

For Nhial's sake, I hope the conflict in South Sudan ends soon. Nhial deserves a chance at a peaceful life in the country she is determined to help.

Her story also shows how much damage war does to education. When war ravages a nation, schools close down or children fear leaving their homes to walk to school. This brings the education rate down for refugee children, meaning that many get no education at all.

Nhial did not get any formal education until she reached Kakuma. For the children currently in South Sudan, education is rare. Seventy per cent of South Sudanese children aged six to seventeen have never attended school.

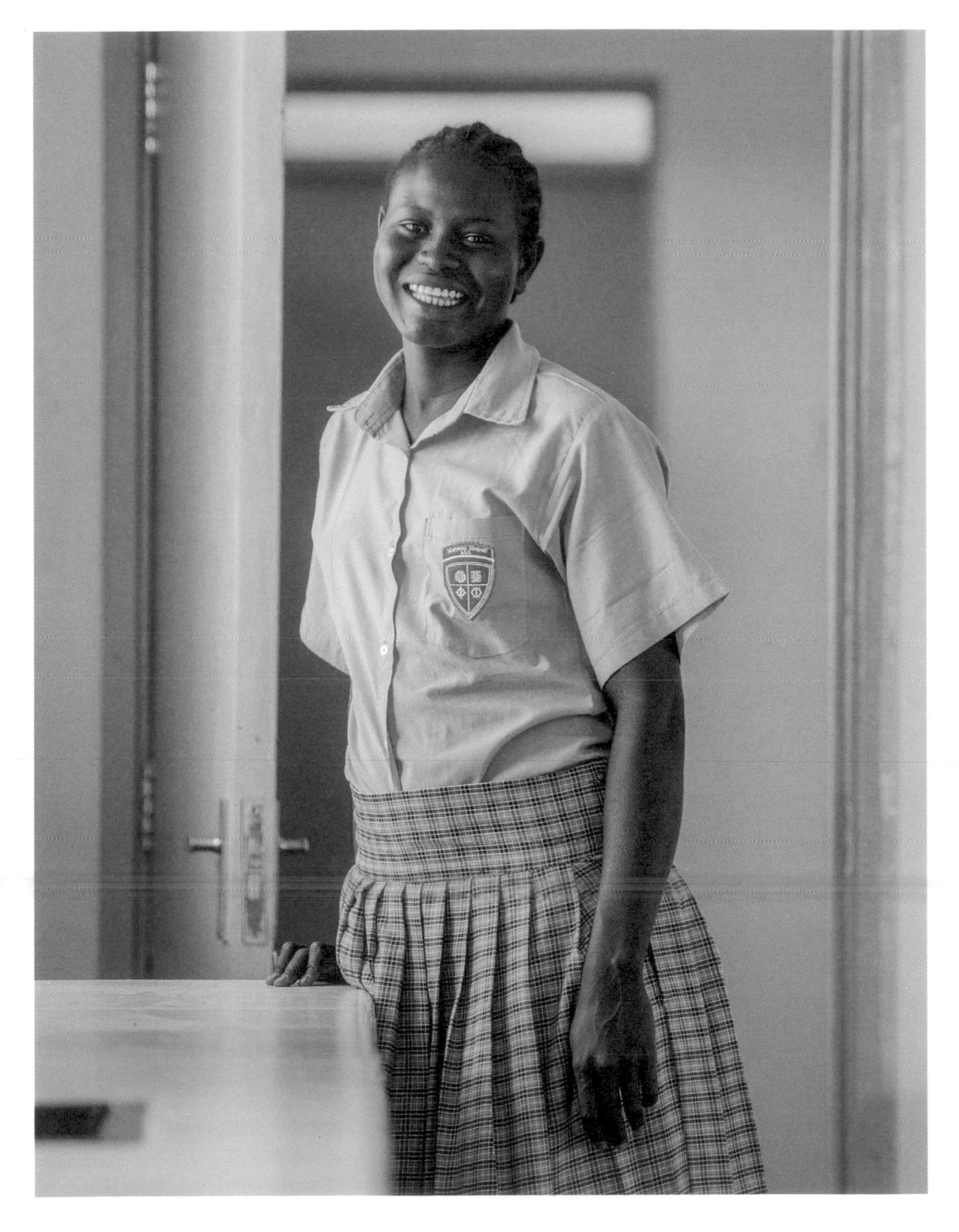

Amach Mabior Kuai

My worst part in the camp is when I am called a refugee. I feel like the world has turned its back on me, but I persevere because life is all about perseverance.

My name is Amach Mabior Kuai (people also call me Ramzy Jay/Alfa Mai). My name, Amach, means like fire. I was born on December 19, 1996 at home. My parents were present during my birth, but my grandparents were absent. I have five siblings aged fifteen, twelve, nine, six, and three.

"My name, Amach, means like fire."

My family is not that able. But we cope with life because the situation will change one day. My parents are all alive. My family is polygamous. My mom is the first wife. I have aunts and uncles, and a lot of cousins from both sides. We are all living here except my father, who is in South Sudan with his other wife.

I am from South Sudan. My country is the youngest independent country in Africa. It got independence on July 9, 2011. I have been living in Kakuma since my birth. Our house is made of mud and iron sheets, and in a strong wind, the iron sheets can be carried away.

At times it floods during rainstorms. It is a stressful life but we have to bear it.

My village is the happiest place to be even now. A lot of people are not educated so they usually do things informally. But that is a way of expressing ourselves. We used to have our traditional dances on Thursdays and Sundays, and these were very admirable. The number of people who live in my village is about a half million.

My nursery school life was fantastic. I enjoyed playing and interacting with my fellow pupils. My primary school was quite good because I was able to learn the world with its continents and was able to know that there are other people existing apart from those from our continent.

I am still living in Kakuma now. My best friend is Becky Awan. She deserves that name because she is always there for me in worst and best times of my life. My other friends in the camp are Tabitha Adhieu, Mary Alek, Rebecca Akur and Suzy Anyier.

We do practice our religion in the camp. Religion is very important in my life because at the moment I believe in Christ; this gives me hope for my future. It makes me feel that everything is possible. We practice our religion by praising and worshipping the Lord and spreading His word.

"I hope that one day I will no longer be called a refugee but a citizen."

My life in Kakuma is not that simple, but also it's not too bad, because a life without bends in the road is never a good life. What we experience now will change us in preparation for the future.

My worst part in the camp is when I am called a refugee. I feel like the world has turned its back on me, but I persevere because life is all about perseverance.

The best part of life in the camp is when I am studying so I can accomplish what I hope to. The obstacles to my ambition are mostly health-related. My health is not that good.

I suffer from some diseases that disturb me a lot, like ulcers and typhoid.

Those who join Morneau Shepell School are the girls with the best grades in the camp. I am in grade 11 there. My favourite subjects are geography, mathematics, and physics. I also like English because it is an international language. I love Physics because my career depends on it. I try my best.

The classes are tough, but nothing can be done about it other than working harder. My teachers are the best teachers. They really sacrifice their time in order for us to pass. They do everything they can to make sure we become successful people in life.

I would like to do petroleum engineering. I am working towards going to university. I would like to go to Canada for further studies. I would like to live in my homeland when I grow older. I always hope that my future will one day change to a better one.

I hope that one day I will no longer be called a refugee but a citizen.

Clare: I love that Amach has a nickname. So do some of my girlfriends. Sometimes I think we have so much in common, and we do (like music, pop culture, interest in school). But then I think that Amach was born in Kakuma and has been living there for her entire life.

Amach's life is representative of so many refugees who live in what is called a prolonged refugee situation. Being born in a refugee camp can be both a blessing and a curse. Amach has never experienced war in her country of origin, but she has also never lived in the country her family came from. She identifies with a place she has never seen. This type of protracted refugee situation can cause real identity crises. Refugees live their whole life not being Kenyan but also not feeling like they belong to any other nationality.

This situation can also lead to a profound sense of hopelessness. How can anyone hope to find a permanent home when all they have ever known is a refugee camp? Amach's sense of home and the world outside of Kakuma has come entirely from stories told by her family, friends, and fellow South Sudanese—she can only imagine.

Esther Nyakong

I have so many questions. Why is
Canada peaceful? Why is it a great country?
Is there racism in Canada? Are there black
people like me? How are your politicians?
How do you make peace?

My name is Esther Nyakong. I was born on
April 10, 1998 in Juba, the capital of South
Sudan. My mom gave birth to me at home with
the help of my grandmother, who passed on
when I was still very young. I was told that she
died of shock when she heard that my dad,
her son, was killed in the war.

**"I am a girl full of confidence,
determination, and hard work.
I will do my best to achieve my
dream. I love talking, laughing,
and cracking jokes, and I love
people equally."**

I have two sisters, Sylvia (twenty-one) and
Teresa (nineteen). My family is a single-parent
family. My mom was my dad's only wife. I have
aunts, uncles, and cousins.

My country is very corrupt, with a lot of
injustices. It is a very sorrowful and tearful
country and people are killed there every day.
The country does not have peace amongst
the communities.

Throughout my life, I have never settled in
one place. My mom, siblings, and I have always
moved from place to place searching for security, food, shelter, and clothing.

Our house was made of mud and grass-
thatching. My village was actually a fearful place

because people had no peace among themselves. They lived as enemies. In my village, the
population was approximately 120,000 people.

Life became too difficult for us. Apart from
the basic needs that were not being met, we
also lacked security. Every sunrise and sunset
we could hear gunshots from every corner, and
we knew our lives were at risk. My former
home was destroyed.

We moved from Juba to a place called Yei,
but there things were worse. At times we could
even go for two to three days without food,
walking barefoot and wearing tattered clothes.
We then moved from Yei to Abei, but there we
almost lost our lives. There was no security. The
journey was very tiresome, full of hunger and
thirst. As we moved, we never carried anything
edible. I missed much from school. And we
continued moving until when we came to discover a camp in Kenya by the name of Kakuma,
and with the help of the United Nations, they
provided us with food, shelter, security, and
even clothing.

Due to movement from one place to another,
I have gone to different schools. My first school
was Liberty Primary School and my second was
Rainbow Academy, where I was made to repeat
classes because my head was blank due to moving from place to place. I had not been reading
for long. I schooled there for about a year and
then we moved again.

I stayed again for two years without attending school. Then I joined Shambe Primary School. In all the schools I have been to, the classes have been congested and some pupils have been sitting on the floor, while others were standing at the back as the teachers taught. The teachers were good and friendly. They tried their best to attend classes and gave us what we required.

My favourite subjects are biology, chemistry, physics and math. I like them because they are my career subjects and they are also easy to understand. I do perform well in class.

My family and I came to Kakuma for various reasons. As I mentioned earlier, my dad died when I was very young and my mom was left with all the responsibility of feeding, schooling, and sheltering us, which became so difficult for her since she does not work anywhere and is illiterate.

The first days in the camp were difficult and hard to cope with due to the climate, but with time we got used to it. Temperatures here reach about 37–40°C.

I have friends who are both boys and girls because I am so social with people. I have friends from around my community and also outside. We practice our religion in the camp by coming together and worshipping God. Religion is very important to me because it brings me close to God and helps me to understand Him better. I practice my religion by going to church every Sunday, reading the Bible, and praying.

My best moments are when I am in school learning, whereas my worst moments are when am at home doing nothing.

The schools in the camp are a bit difficult and challenging to cope with. Students walk long distances to school every morning and back home. Also when they go home, they have house chores and have no time to conduct personal studies. I got to Morneau Shepell Secondary through hard work and determination. Many girls wish to be in the school but they do not get the opportunity.

I am a grade-A student. Classes are difficult because we have eleven subjects to deal with. I have a best friend by the name Grace Nyibol; dark, short and plump. The teachers are kind and friendly, and they sacrifice their own weekends to come to school to teach us.

"You are the one who shapes your life. You are the one who makes your life a success."

This is my seventh year in Kakuma. A lot of people from my home are also in the camp. I live with my relatives here. My life in the camp is better than when I was in my homeland, but I do face some challenges here. My whole family is not with me; my mom went back to Sudan. Currently my siblings and I are living with our relatives.

It has always been my dream to become a neurosurgeon. When I complete my secondary school education, I would like to enroll in a very nice university in Canada. I would like to study medicine. After I accomplish my dreams of becoming a neurosurgeon, I wish to have children. I hope my future will be successful and I will live happily with my husband and children.

The obstacles to me doing what I want in the future are lack of support facilities at home and at school. Otherwise I am a girl full of confidence, determination, and hard work. I will do my best to achieve my dream. I love talking, laughing, and cracking jokes, and I love people equally.

You are the one who shapes your life. You are the one who makes your life a success.

Clare: I can't wait to meet Esther. She is so compelling and riveting I can't help but want to be around her, to exist in her world. Even in her writing and in photos she has this charismatic presence that makes me want to learn more about her and laugh with her. She strikes me as a person who lives for the moment and has the rare ability to find joy, no matter how hard life is.

Esther is a striker on the school soccer team. She adores soccer, but she is not just an athlete. She is an intensely intellectual and inquisitive human being who questions everyone and everything around her.

Esther speaks like a seasoned philosopher. She intuitively knows when to crack a joke to turn a serious situation into a comedic one.

She transformed what could have been a serious photo shoot with Jjumba into an amusing one by staging a mock science experiment.

Because Esther goes to Morneau Shepell, she is fascinated by Canadians and their culture. She desperately wants to understand other countries, and she takes every opportunity to ask questions to get a sense of what life is like outside of her experiences in South Sudan and Kakuma.

After an immensely difficult life, Esther has managed to become an inspirational person. She has seen the horrors of war and violence in South Sudan. If anything, her terrifying past has made her wise beyond her years, leaving her with a desire for knowledge and a determination to create a better life for herself.

Sarah Nyajuok Gik

We South Sudanese are really behind, so in my country I want to improve my lifestyle and not have the fighting that is happening there. I want to be educated.

My name is Sarah Nyajuok Gik. I was born on January 1, 1996 in South Sudan, in a village called Kiech Kuon. I was born at home in my late grandmother's hut. Both parents were present at my birth. I stayed with my father for only three years after I was born. I have two sisters, Nyaloki (fourteen) and Nyaruot (nine).

My family is polygamous—my father had three wives apart from my mother. During the war, we were all separated and my mother never knew where the co-wives went after my father was killed. My family life is not that good now since my mother is unable to satisfy all my and my siblings' needs.

"I got to Kakuma when my mother was gunned down after my late father died during the disruption by the SPLM army."

My mother told me I might have living aunts, uncles, and cousins together with the rest of my father's family in South Sudan. But since the war broke out, she does not know where they are. She is not sure whether they are still alive or not.

My religion is important since I believe that through God's protection, I can exist through my challenges. I practice my religion by helping old people in the community, participating in church activities such as services, choir practices, and some manual work in the church, such as cleaning.

My country of origin is South Sudan. My country is comprised of sixty-four tribes and ten states. South Sudan is a newborn country, having achieved independence on July 9, 2013. It has a lot of inequality, corruption among leaders, tribalism, and nepotism.

I have never stayed in a place that can be called a permanent home. I only stayed in Nasir for a month. Our temporary house was my late grandparents' hut. Nasir was densely populated, and people lived in huts made from grass. The village had a small town within it with only Arabs. It was very hard for people to get what they needed since there was a language barrier. The main economic activity was fishing since the people are River Lake Nilotes where the Blue Nile passes through the village.

Most people in the village were women and children since men didn't stay in one place. Many of those men were soldiers and some died during the war. There were a large number of widows and orphan children in the village.

There was lack of peace and there was also a lot of displacement in the country, with people being killed like chickens.

I came to Kakuma because of war in my country. I got to Kakuma when my mother was gunned down after my late father died during

the disruption by the SPLM army. She was then brought to Lokichogio in Kenya by the Red Cross. At the hospital, together with other wounded people, my mother couldn't believe she and her child could be alive since she was shot while seven months pregnant. By good luck the child was safe in the womb.

After about two months in the hospital, she delivered through Cesarean since her body was paralyzed. She was then given crutches with which to support herself. She left me alone in Sudan where I didn't know anyone. I was then taken by a neighbour, a friend of my mother, who agreed to care for me. My mother was brought back from Lokichogio then taken to a hospital in Nasir. She stayed there for more than a year without me knowing. She really suffered since there was no one to look after her and the baby.

Some months later, she sent many people to look for me. The woman I stayed with heard that my mother was back in Kenya. She took me to her. We stayed with my mother, who helplessly depended on hospital meals. The newborn didn't have any clothing to put on. My mother's only hope was prayer because she had no relatives or friends, nor a husband.

When she was discharged from hospital, we had no place to stay, so we returned to the hospital. The people of the Red Cross helped by building us a small hut in the hospital.

My mother was powerless, as she was on crutches. The meals were not frequent; maybe once a day.

After three months the UNHCR Agency came to the hospital to look after the sick people. They found us in that small hut. They felt pity for us and helped my mother. After some months, they brought us to Kakuma Refugee Camp. The trip to Kakuma was very hard. We stayed in Kakuma with only the support of UNHCR. We have now been in Kakuma for eleven years. My life is just full of sorrow; no happiness at all.

My first school in Kakuma Refugee Camp was Fuji Primary School. I had never attended school in my country of origin. There were so many children in this school. As the number of the pupils was too large, we never had an opportunity to look into a textbook nor to touch it.

I struggled until I finished my class four in Fuji Primary School, where I sometimes went barefoot. At the end of term, I was called out as the best girl and was then told to go to a boarding school supported by the Lutheran World Federation. Since my mother couldn't provide for me, the children's rights staff cared for me. The school was called Angelina Jolie Primary School. It was quite good. Since the school was free, the only stress sometimes was where to get basic supplies, such as lotions, pens, and

Sarah poses before a fashion show that is part of the cultural performance.
Alek Wek, the British supermodel who fled South Sudan at age 14, is one of her role models.

sandals. We stayed for three months since it is a boarding school. The main holidays were April, August, and December.

I joined high school in 2013 at Somali Bantu Secondary School, a mixed day school. I wished to go to a boarding school, and God must have heard my prayers, since I was brought to Morneau Shepell Secondary School for Girls in 2014. I am in senior three now. My favourite subject is geography.

"Going to school also makes you believe your dreams can come true in the future."

The life is not that good in the camp since I do not have any support apart from UNHCR. I depend on what they give in rations. My mother really tried, but could not help much. She is disabled so she can't walk for a long distance.

My first day in the camp seemed bad, but it has become a better place since there is peace and free education. I'm still living in Kakuma Refugee Camp since I have nowhere to go—my country is not yet peaceful and I don't have any relatives in Sudan.

In the camp I interact with friends, regardless of my background and my life challenges. They help me in my times of difficulties. I love them so much.

My best part of living in camp is getting an education and interacting with my teachers and fellow students. Although the camp may expose you to some difficulties in life, going to school also makes you believe your dreams can come true in future. It gives me hope in life. The school days are the best days in my life.

MSSSG has helped so many girls in the camp since most of the camp schools are day schools and some girls are not able to walk that far since they face different challenges. Some don't have parents or relatives, and some are denied the chance to attend school by their parents so they can marry instead. Many students drop out due to such challenges.

I would like to become a pilot in the future. I also dream of being a fashion model. Indeed, I will make my dreams come true through further education in university. I would like to go to university in Canada immediately after I am done with my secondary education. In university, I would like also to do a little bit of human physical geography.

When I grow older, I would like to be in a place where I can live well and make sure my children can study, too. I would like to have children after my further studies or after I'm done with my dreams. In life I would help those who are disadvantaged in life: for example, educating orphans. Indeed I would like to be like Morneau Shepell, giving services to the unfortunate.

Clare: From 1983 to 2005, conflict raged between North and South Sudan. It was during this time, as Sarah mentioned, that her father was killed.

Sarah was ten years old when she first went to school. She never attended school before fleeing to Kenya. In South Sudan, only 16 per cent of girls are literate, so it is not surprising that Sarah had no education prior to arriving in Kakuma Refugee Camp.

Sarah says that school uniforms are often a source of pride in the refugee camp, so the lack of uniforms for many makes the students sad. If students can't afford uniforms or theirs are torn, girls especially will miss school. Uniforms make students feel like they are equal to all of their peers, no matter their background. They are also a material way for the students to show off the fact that they are attending school.

School uniforms can also be a source of pride in Canada and at Havergal College. Your school uniform shows who you are, and where you belong. Although Havergal students sometimes grow tired of wearing a uniform, they are proud to wear green and gold, their school colours, at sporting events and extracurricular competitions.

Even though Sarah started school late, she did well and was able to go to Angelina Jolie Primary School. It opened in 2005 through a donation made by UNHCR Ambassador Angelina Jolie. A boarding school for girls recognized for their performance and their vulnerability, Angelina Jolie Primary School was a model for MSSSG when it was being conceived. Now several girls who went to Angelina Jolie, not a far walk from MSSSG, go to MSSSG.

Sarah and her family have a tough road ahead. Her mother is a widow and unwell and Sarah has two younger sisters who also dream of leaving Kakuma. It has been eleven years since Sarah and her family reached Kakuma Refugee Camp. She has no way to return home because South Sudan is not yet peaceful.

There is currently also intense fighting between the Nuer and the Dinka. Although South Sudan celebrated when it finally gained independence from Sudan, violence erupted again just two years later. This fighting rapidly revealed the fragility of the state of calm that South Sudan had rested in following its independence. Many fled South Sudan and journeyed into neighbouring countries. Even today more South Sudanese refugees are continuing to come to Kakuma.

At home with Sarah
Carol Devine

Sarah is friendly, not shy. She models naturally for the camera when Jjumba takes her photo in the long red party dress she wore for the cultural show at the school. Sarah is tall in black high heels. She's a little subdued when we arrive at her home. It's made of wood slats and plastic sheeting walls with a canvas roof, and it looks so fragile. We enter through a gate made of sticks, perhaps bamboo. I wonder how

Sarah feels. Happy to see her family? Slightly awkward that these five people have shown up unexpectedly at her home? She doesn't seem uncomfortable, but she is quiet, maybe slowly observing and taking it all in. I think how I would feel if my son or daughter unexpectedly brought home five international guests.

Sarah goes in first to give her mom the heads-up that we are here.

We are in the courtyard, a rectangular block with a few other mud buildings, presumably a kitchen, and perhaps a living quarter. One long building has a pretty design on it of a flower in earth tones. On each side of this plot of land are other small rectangular compounds.

Sarah invites us in and her mother, younger sister, a family friend, and another child say hello to us. All are tall like Sarah. Her mom, slight and frail, has a kerchief in her hair. She smiles at us. Sarah's mom speaks no English. Sarah's family members disappear one by one while Sarah brings in colourful plastic chairs for us to sit on. Our hosts are gracious.

Inside one of the rooms in Sarah's small family compound it is hot. It's not quite a round *tukul* like the homes I saw in South Sudan, but it reminds me of that—a dirt floor, plastic cups, flowered mattresses. Sunlight comes in through slits in the walls. Sarah's family is extremely poor and I imagine lives like most in Kakuma camp do, but perhaps faces extra challenges, as Sarah's mother is unwell.

It's a lovely moment—Sarah's family arrives back soon in nice dresses. Sarah's little sister is wearing a red-and-white polka dot dress. Her mom is wearing a two-tone teal dress. Sarah's sister is leaning on the pole that holds up the middle of the structure, watching everything. Mohamud asks her where she goes to school. She says she attends Fuji Primary School, right on the other side of the wide dusty road we came on. He asks if she wants to go to Morneau Shepell, and she smiles. "Yes," she says.

Mohamud and I introduce ourselves. Sarah's mom, using Sarah as a translator, thanks Mohamud for the opportunity for Sarah to study at Morneau Shepell. Suddenly three boys arrive who are sharply but casually dressed. Someone says that they are Lost Boys. One is visiting from Uganda, where he is studying. This terrific news, I'm sure, inspires others to believe it's possible to leave Kakuma to reach better opportunities. I loved how the boys just dropped in. Was it happenstance or did someone let them know we were there?

Sarah disappears now and one of the young men translates for us. I'm not listening so much to what the boy is saying. I'm listening to Sarah's mom's voice and tone, and watching her face. Sarah attending MSSSG is a source of pride, happiness, and hope for her mother. For the first time, despite listening to the girls' struggles and stories for two days, I am feeling emotional. I know Sarah's mother was shot in the war when she was pregnant and that she lost her husband.

This family unit is dignified and stalwart, but it feels as if they are teetering on an edge. I wonder how different their existence is from how it would be in South Sudan. There is no war here, but they are not home. I am indignant that a family should have to suffer so much.

Sudan

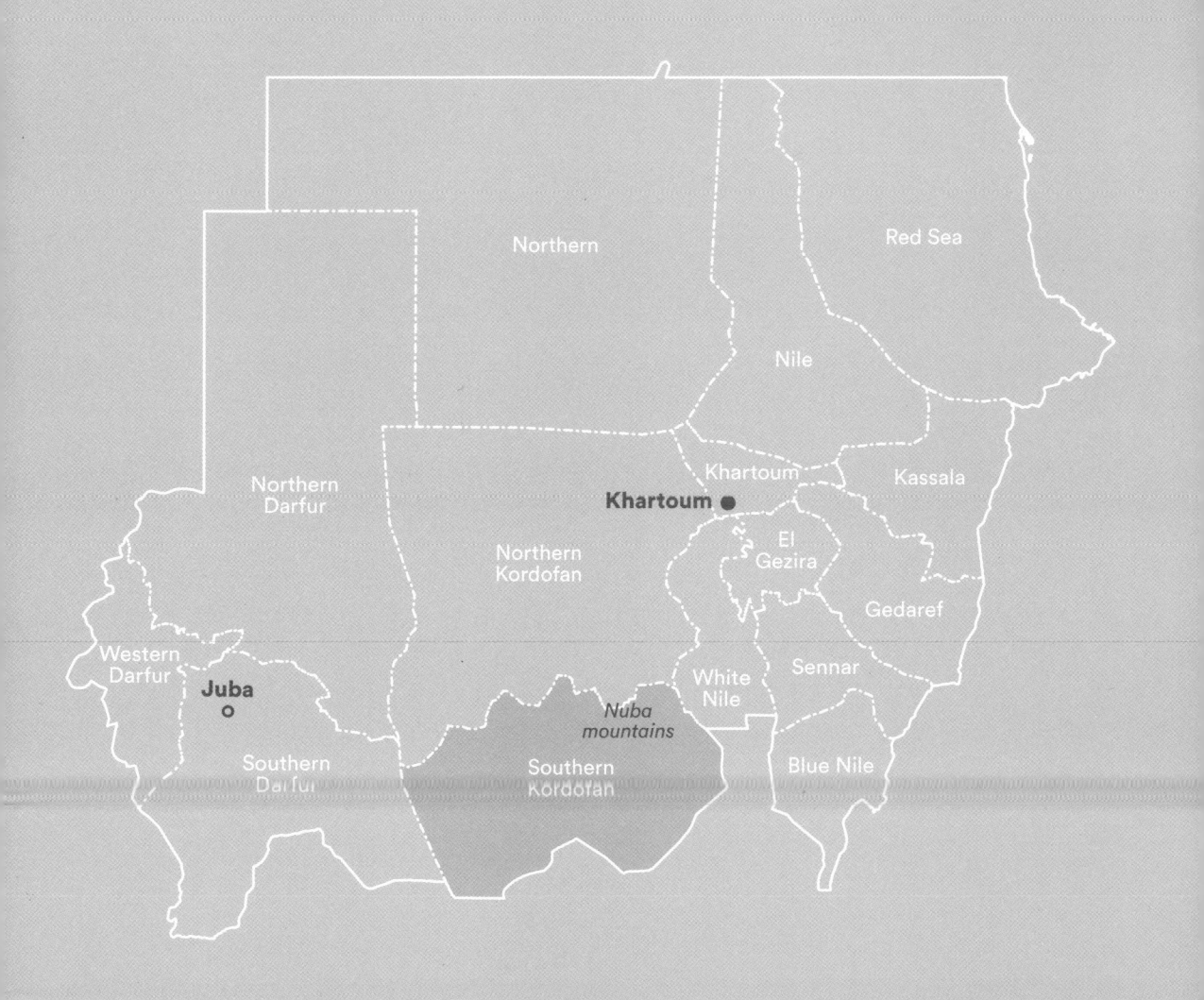

Northern

Red Sea

Nile

Northern
Darfur

Khartoum

Kassala

Khartoum ●

Northern
Kordofan

El
Gezira

Gedaref

Western
Darfur

Juba
○

*Nuba
mountains*

White
Nile

Sennar

Southern
Darfur

Southern
Kordofan

Blue Nile

Zahira Habila Ariss

My country of origin is Sudan.
It was the largest country on the African
continent but is now divided into two:
North and South Sudan.

My name is Zahira Habila Ariss. I was born in August 1996 in a village surrounded by mountains. My birth was traditional because by then there were no hospitals due to war. People survived on herbs for medication. Both my parents were alive then, but my grandparents were not present during my birth.

I am the eighth-born of nine children. I have four brothers and three sisters who are living, but two of my siblings died at their birth. I also have three other siblings from my stepmother. My three elder brothers are married and have kids. So I have a very large extended family.

My country of origin is Sudan. It was the largest country on the African continent but is now divided into two: North and South Sudan. I am from North Sudan. My country is semi-arid. Temperatures are usually very high, extending up to 40°C.

Unfortunately, my father died in 2004 due to a stroke, but my mother is alive. My family is polygamous. My father had two wives but the second one was divorced and left three kids who live with us. I have two uncles and two aunts who bore me several cousins, both male and female.

My religion is Christianity and it is important in my life. I usually practice it by praying, singing, worshipping, and praising God. I usually try to attend every activity concerning my religion.

Since my birth, I lived in my home country and I never found a chance to leave her for even one month. It was 2013 when I left for Kakuma. I lived in South Korodofan State, one of the Northern Sudan areas. My house was a temporary shelter because our place was ruined in war and permanent houses were unheard of.

My home village is in a rocky place with a lot of bushes around. Most of our economic activities were agricultural, since the place was fertile. We lived as a well-united community neighbouring one another.

After a very long regime of war the Sudanese Comprehensive Peace Agreement was signed and schools were opened to educate the children. But before that, there were no schools. That was when I was registered in a school just next to our home. The schools were taught by Kenyan teachers imported to offer services in our place because we had no professional teachers in our country.

The school I attended was highly populated with about 2,000 pupils. They were from different villages surrounding the school. In the whole region we had only one school for all the children.

The number of boys was higher compared to girls. This is because girls' education was discouraged in my place. We had no uniforms. We could wear any clothes we had. During those times, we had no school materials. In the entire school we had two or three textbooks per subject. They could only be used by the teachers but not pupils. Computers were not available. Even teachers themselves never had a chance to use them.

"That was when my cousin and I made up our minds to leave for an unknown place. We parted from our families. We set out in a direction that we did not know, unsure where it would lead us."

I usually attended school at home daily unless I was sick. I only missed school one or two days per year. My favourite subject was science. I liked it because it dealt with animals' lives. I did well in class.

War broke out for the second time as a result of unfair elections of the leaders. The oppressed had to fight for their rights. Life became terrible and one could not bear it. We left our homes and flew into mountains for safety. But still the mountains did not protect us or the locals. People scattered to all the parts they could find safety and survival.

That was when my cousin and I made up our minds to leave for an unknown place. We parted from our families. We set out in a direction that we did not know, unsure where it would lead us.

We journeyed for seven days on foot in the depths of forests. After a long and tiresome journey, we came to a place where some people accommodated us. We found it unsafe.

We decided to continue with our journeying. By good luck, we found a truck that was heading to Kakuma Refugee Camp and we were given a lift. It took three days to arrive in Kakuma. After that we reached the Reception Centre where we were attended to.

I have now only been in Kakuma for two years and six months. I only missed school for one year.

It is unfortunate that I am only with my cousin. The rest of my family members are in my home country. We don't know their whereabouts.

My first days in Kakuma were not enjoyable because I was not familiar with the environment and I was sad I'd left all my people behind. I was worried and always stressed. I had no friends or relatives except my cousin. But after some time, I made several friends who comforted me. Several of my friends already have children. I will be happy to be a mom, but later.

Life now in Kakuma is a little bit favourable because I busy myself with school and spend most of my time with friends. I have forgotten what transpired in my past life. I am now boarding at Morneau Shepell Secondary School for Girls, where all my needs are provided for.

After completing my secondary education, I am hoping to go to university if I get a chance. My wish is to be anywhere as long as I am learning. I wish to study medicine at the university.

After my schooling, I wish to live in any part of the globe as long as it is suitable and I am together with my family. I plan to have children in the future. I hope my future will be bright and fruitful and I can enjoy all sorts of things that I need in life.

The possible obstacle to my dreams and wishes is that I might not find money to pay for university fees. The fact that I am a refugee and I am alone, I may not find a sponsor.

Clare: Zahira was born into a war-torn country. Sudan was originally under British-Egyptian rule, and for a long time was considered a part of Egypt, sharing its rich history with ancient Egypt. Sudan gained its independence from Egypt in 1956. Peace in this new country didn't last long. The start of Sudan's first civil war was in 1956, some say minutes after gaining independence from Egypt. This civil war between the north and south of Sudan lasted for almost two decades, ending in 1972 when the south of Sudan was granted autonomy.

Conflict started again in 1983, with renewed fighting between the north and south. Zahira grew up during this second civil war and spent the first nine years of her life amid intense conflict. Hospitals were destroyed or looted. If anyone got sick or injured, he or she may not have survived, as they were forced to use natural herbs as medication. Herbal medication can prevent and heal some illnesses but it is no match for bullet wounds. Lack of medical care was part of the reason for the massive death toll of Sudan's two civil wars of over two million people.

Zahira survived in Sudan until 2013, when she decided that she could not live as she was living anymore.

After attacks on her village, Zahira's family was forced to flee their home to the mountains for safety. Zahira had to leave her school and abandon any hope of education in the future in order to stay alive.

Unfortunately, the mountains offered no safety for Zahira and her family. The Nuba Mountains mark the border between Sudan and South Sudan; the latter gained its independence in 2011. Villagers living in the Nuba Mountains in Sudan are a mix of Christians and Muslims who believe they can co-exist peacefully. This created conflict in Sudan because much of the rest of Sudan is Muslim, and the government does not seem to have to the same view of religious tolerance.

The Nuba Mountains are also a home to a rebel army that is supported by local people. The government has strategically bombed rebels in the Nuba Mountains, destroying civilian villages and killing innocent people, all in an attempt to make the area uninhabitable. Essentially, the Sudanese government is trying to kill all of its civilians living in the Nuba Mountains so that they can no longer support rebels.

Life in the Nuba Mountains is extraordinarily hard. Not only do civilians live with the bombing, but the government cut them off from all resources, meaning they have no access to medicine and food from outside of their villages. This has been going on for so long that children have learned to identify the sounds of different bombs.

While there is some improvement in the security situation in Darfur, profound political and environmental challenges mean the situation is fragile.

The Reception Centre Zahira speaks of is a large compound with L-shaped buildings to the left of the gate, a large field and a long row of large temporary structures for incoming refugees. Any refugee that arrives in Kakuma has to spend several days in the Reception Centre to be screened and processed, and to wait until they are assigned accommodation in the camp.

Many of the girls in Kakuma tell me it's an important place in the camp because it represents their first point of arrival, but also where it sank in that they'd arrived to a new and indefinite "home."

Somalia

Awdal

Woqooyi
Galbeed

Sanaag

Bari

Togdheer

Sool

Nugaal

Mudug

Galguduud

Bakool

Hiiraan

Gedo

Shabeellaha
Dhexe

Bay

Warta Nabada District

Jubbada
Dhexe

Mogadishu

Shabeellahda
Hoose

Jubbada
Hoose

Lula Abdulkhadir Modhar

As the firstborn child I have to be
an example to my siblings, especially
my sisters. I give my family hope.

My name is Lula Abdulkhadir Modhar. I was born in Jomvu (Mombasa) on February 1, 1998 at home with both my parents. My grandparents were already dead by then.

I am the first born in my family, followed by my sisters Amina, who is fourteen, Hanan, thirteen, Sharifa, eleven, and my two brothers, Hassan and Hussein, who are nine and seven years old.

We are a nuclear family. I live with both my parents. We are a monogamous family. I don't know about my aunts', uncles' or cousins' whereabouts since my parents left them in Somalia during the war sixteen years ago.

My country is Somalia, though I was born in Mombasa. In Kakuma the temperatures are very high during the day and low at night. Sometimes it rains so heavily our houses are carried away by floods. We live in a house built of bricks and covered by some boxes and *makuti* (thatching made from dry coconut palm). Our village in Kakuma Camp is congested. There are about 600 people living here.

I started my preschool in Kakuma. The schools were crowded and lacked benches for sitting. The textbooks were also insufficient. I borrowed and returned them at the end of the day. The number of children that went to my school was approximately 700 boys and 500 girls. Attending school every day is what I like, so the only days I missed was when I was sick or when the seasonal rivers prevented me from accessing school.

We learned social studies, math, English, Kiswahili, and science. I like mathematics because of calculations that involve playing with numbers and science because I want to discover more things about living organisms. I did well in class.

My life in Kakuma is not easy. Sometimes homes are invaded and attacked by robbers. People lose their lives. My friends in the camp are Leila, Habiba, Cathrine, Zeinab, Adut and many others, including my best friend, Rhodha. She is good and kindhearted. She always tells the truth and corrects me whenever she knows I am wrong. She is also a responsible girl.

My religion is more important in my life than anything else. I am a Muslim and I pray five times a day. The first prayer is early in the morning, followed by an afternoon prayer, an evening prayer, a late evening prayer, and finally a night prayer. These are essential in Islam. I also fast during the holy month (Ramadhan).

Our teachers are good and hardworking. They are always ready to help when we go for consultations. They are also good advisors, who always inspire us.

In the future I would like to be a doctor. After my form four I would like to go to Canada and study medicine. After university, I want to live in Canada, marry, and have children. I hope to have a bright future. I would like to have my own job and be independent so that I can help my family and other people who are in need.

Clare: Lula and people living in Kakuma have a strong desire to be relocated. Many refugees are hopeful that they will be resettled to countries such as the United States and Canada, as they see the Western world as a better place to live. As some of the refugees attend schools that are funded by donors in North America, it seems like a good place to go for further education.

Somalia is troubled by constant fighting, attacks by the terrorist group Al-Shabaab, piracy off the Somali coast, and famines.

For Lula's family, who has spent sixteen years in the refugee camp, it is hard to be hopeful that they will find their way out of the camp to a better life. They once managed to fly to Nairobi, Kenya, on their way to relocate to the United States, but were turned around because of a technicality in the immigration papers. Before leaving, the Modhars gave away everything they had, including their home. They wanted to give what little they had to others who needed it more, as they would surely have enough in their new life in the United States. This made the journey back to Kakuma camp distressing for the Modhar family. They had to reconstruct their entire life upon their return.

"We had to come back from Nairobi when we couldn't go to the US anymore, though we thought we were about to all leave. It was because of a missing fingerprint or something for my brother. I can remember the exact day and hour when we had to return to Kakuma. It was devastating. To this day I am stressed when I hear the sound of planes or learn someone is going away with IOM [International Organization for Migration]. We had given away every single possession, had done our medical checks, had prepared for a new life. I want to leave here," Lula said.

Lula and her family's dream of resettlement remains strong but cautious. Unfortunately, this is not uncommon in Kakuma Refugee Camp; many refugees have been in Kakuma for over twenty years, and no longer hold onto hope that they will be relocated to another country or be able to return to their home country.

Although her mother works hard to help her family out, Lula is accustomed to depending on the UNHCR, WFP, and other aid organizations for support.

Lula has survived in Kakuma Refugee Camp with her six siblings, her ill father, and her hardworking mother. As the oldest child of six, Lula feels immense responsibility because her entire family is depending on her for a brighter future. However, this is a burden Lula accepts, feeling proud that she can do something to help her family. She gives her family hope. Lula wants to change her family's situation and help them leave Kakuma and Kenya for the United States or Canada.

Although the refugees living in Kakuma Refugee Camp receive assistance from aid organizations and are safe from being sent back to their countries of origin, they are trapped in the camp. Refugees are not able to move freely outside of the camp and cannot easily obtain an education or employment outside the camp. The lack of freedom can cause refugees to feel undignified and unable to control their lives. It is very difficult for many refugees such as Lula, because although their families are safer than they were prior to arriving in Kakuma Refugee Camp, they are stuck in a place that does not feel like a permanent settlement.

Lula is an amazing student and young woman. She is determined, independent, and adaptable. She has persevered through each and every challenge that life has thrown her way, and is determined to continue to do so until she achieves her dreams.

A visit with the Modhar Family
Carol Devine

After the visit to Sarah's family we all go to meet Lula's family. Lula's home is long and narrow with a private outhouse at the right of the 'front door' which is a corrugated tin swing gate. The first room off a long open-roofed corridor is a common room, a living room perhaps also where many family members sleep. The floor is covered with linoleum-patterned mock tiles on top of the ground—a step up in comfort from Sarah's mom's dirt floor. But Lula tells us during the rainy season their place floods like everyone else's. The "wall" is made of UNHCR woven plastic bags spread out like tarps with Arabic writing on them in black and red marker. I wish I'd asked what it said. The home is across from the local mosque, and we can hear, on a loud speaker, someone humming.

There's a formality to Lula's dad and also a warmth—he smiles and greets all of us but only shakes Mohamud's hand. He invites us to sit in the living area. We remove our shoes and sit on mattresses pushed in the corners. He and Mohamud speak amicably in Somali; they have met before. Mohamud translates for us. Lula's youngest sister stands against the white wall next to her sister. Her younger brother comes in and out of the room. The youngest sister gives a kind of speech in English on the importance of education and its ability to change circumstances. She acknowledges, like Lula has, how Lula as the firstborn must encourage the younger siblings to "do their level best at school." The sister is confident, and passionate, though she is only about twelve. I imagine her addressing the UN.

Mohamud asks if she wants to go to Morneau Shepell like her older sisters. She surprises us by saying she wants to go to another school.

Mohamud smiles and explains—she wants to go to the top school not in Kakuma but in Kenya.

Lula's dad is proud of his family. I can see it in the pride he shows when he listens to his children. He leaves for a moment and fetches a laminated piece of A4 paper. It is his "family photo"—a list of names with small images, presumably the identification paperwork he needed for their unsuccessful move to the US. I think how much the family photos Jjumba will take will mean to the family.

Jjumba prepares to take a photo of the family and suddenly the gate opens. It is Lula's mom and youngest brother with his arm in a cast. She's holding a large envelope, which contains the X-ray, and she has the neighbour's small son with her. When someone tries to shoo him out of the family photo Jjumba is retaking with all the family members, Lula's mom says they must let him stay.

A wonderful surprise happened as we left Lula's family's home to walk to the mosque and then the market. Sarah, who was with us on the visit to Lula's home, suddenly ran into a young man, a tall Muslim guy she plays basketball with. I loved to learn that she plays on a coed team outside of school just as girls in Toronto do.

These youth co-exist as multinational, multifaith refugee women and men living in a crowded camp in the forlorn corner of another country. They are tenacious and impressive.

It was an honor to meet Lula's family and be in their home, as it was to meet Sarah's. People make their homes wherever they are, but I hope these families can one day be citizens of their country or another country where they don't fear their flimsy walls being washed away in a flood. A country where they can work and move freely and stop feeling as if they are in perpetual motion without a clear destination.

Fardosa Ali Hassan

I was born during wartime and grew up in Mogadishu amongst the flying bazookas.

My name is Fardosa Ali Hassan. I was born in Al-Hayat Hospital on September 21, 1996 in Mogadishu, Somalia. At that time both of my parents and grandmother were present. I have three siblings: Mohamed (twenty-three), Farhiya (twenty-one), and Awaale (thirteen). We are a nuclear, monogamous family. All my family members, including my mother and siblings, as well as a maternal aunt and her children, are with me in Kakuma except my father, who was killed by the Al-Shabaab in Mogadishu. May God be with him.

I am a Somali. Somalia is bordered by Kenya to the northeast and it consists of eighteen provinces. It is also known as the Horn of Africa because of its shape. Most Somali people are nomadic pastoralists. Our country was once developing with great promise, but in 1991 civil war broke out. I wish Somalia would go back to peace.

I lived with my parents and siblings in a town called Warta Nabada, which means Lake of Peace. It was near a beach and had very tall ancient buildings. I was told by my mother that some of the buildings were from before the seventh century, and around 100 million people lived there.

We escaped from our homeland because of insecurity. Our former home was written off by a troop called Al-Shabaab. After that experience, my mother decided that we should move to a secure place. We came by bus all the way from Mogadishu to Dadaab. When we arrived, we felt relieved of our anxiety, but my mother was still insecure, and she decided to move farther from Somalia. That is how we came to Kakuma. The trip from Somalia to Kakuma was very tiresome and difficult. I also missed school so much.

"The best part of living in the camp is the continuation of my education and the worst part is when I hear that there is a bomb blast or war in my homeland."

I have many friends and my best friends are Sahara and Maryama. Sahara is very nice and she is also honest. I do practice my religion very well. My religion is important to my life and I do observe Islamic religion by praying five times a day, fasting in the holy month and giving out charity (when I can).

The best part of living in the camp is the continuation of my education and worst part is when I hear that there is a bomb blast or war in my homeland.

Dadaab Refugee Camp in Kenya is the largest refugee camp complex in the world.

Our school, Morneau Shepell, is among the best schools in the country. It has all the facilities required for smooth learning. After my Kenya Certificate of Primary Education (K.C.P.E) results, I went to the Lutheran World Federation and I was told that I had a chance to learn at Morneau Shepell. I like it very much. And the classes are not difficult to me, although many people say that it is quite difficult.

We usually clean the school at 7:30 am. We study our lessons up to 3:30 pm. After that we participate in the school's co-curricular such as games, clubs, and debate. In the evening we study for two and a half hours before going to bed. Our teachers are very interesting, honest, and encouraging.

In the future I want to become a doctor. I want to study at university in the U.K. because I want to pursue a career in medicine. When I grow older I want to live anywhere I feel like living, and I want to have children. I would like to live a very good life so as to provide my family, orphans, and the poor. Now I am working hard so that I achieve my goals and dreams.

Clare: The year Fardosa was born, 1996, was an uneasy one in Mogadishu. The capital city of Somalia has often been the centre of conflict in the country. The economy and government were in shambles following the reign and death of warlord Mohamed Farah Aidid. Hussein Mohamed Farah, Aidid's son, quickly replaced him.

In 1991, after twenty-two years of life under Mohamed Siad Barre, Somalia's presidential dictator, Somalia's government suddenly changed. Barre was rapidly ousted from power in the same way he'd gained it, through a military coup. This coup led to a violent power struggle between various warlords, killing thousands of civilians who were caught in the middle. This fighting turned into what is known as the Somali Civil War, which has traumatized the country to this day. In 1992, UN peacekeeping forces attempted to intervene and help civilians, but were unable to achieve what they had hoped for, and in 1995 they left. The US was briefly involved in the mission to restore peace in Somalia, but left in 1994 after a violent battle with Somali militias.

Although Somalia has had a turbulent past, there seems to be hope on the horizon. In the past year, the food situation in Somalia has slowly improved, with fewer Somalis facing food crises and malnutrition. The government is attempting to regain its footing, and is accepting the voluntary repatriation of Somali refugees. Dadaab, Kenya's other big refugee camp on the other side of the country, has tentatively started to let Somali refugees return home.

Unfortunately, there is no certainty that Somalia can remain stable. Al-Shabaab, a Somali terrorist group, is present in and outside Somalia, and there is still a lot of maritime pirating. Even if Kakuma takes a cue from Dadaab and helps Somali refugees travel back to their country, some refugees may not want to.

What really struck me in Fardosa's story and letters is how proud she is of the vibrant culture and history of Somalia. Although her country has been plagued with war and unstable government for decades, this has not erased its radiance. Despite so much destruction, Somalia's cultural history has not been obliterated, and Fardosa thinks often of that impressive heritage. This makes it easy to understand why so many refugees like Fardosa want to rebuild their countries.

Ethiopia

Tigray

Gonder

Welo

Gojam

Welega

Shewa

Addis Ababa

o **Gambela**

Ilubabor

Arsi

Harerge

Kefa

Bale

Gamo Gofa

Sidamo

Nyimuch Chuol Wel

Though the schools I have gone to were more than one hour from home, we didn't care about walking all the way because our core business was education.

My name is Nyimuch Chuol Wel. I was born in the village of Luel in Ethiopia on November 20, 1997. I am from a monogamous family. My parents and grandmother were present during my birth. I have four siblings; my eldest sister is nowhere to be found, so only three of us remain. The second-born is twenty-two years old; the third-born is twenty years old; I am eighteen; and the last-born is sixteen-years old.

We have lived with our mother since my father passed away. My mother never got married to any other man. I have one cousin, a niece, and a nephew. I have aunts and uncles, but they have passed away and I don't know where others are. I am a Christian and I am proud of my religion.

Back in Luel the houses were made of mud and grass. In our village there were more than five thousand of us, and we had sixty-four tribes. We practiced farming and keeping livestock, although the water source was five kilometers away.

I started using textbooks and wearing a uniform in Angelina Jolie Primary School, where I first started boarding, though I never got a chance to use a computer because they were not there. My favourite subjects are languages. I love those classes because they make me speak fluently and eloquently.

We came to Kakuma after my father was assassinated for supporting the political party that was uniting the citizens to live in peace. Our house was locked and we couldn't return home.

The trip to Kenya was frightening and tiresome because we didn't know exactly where we were going, and to make matters worse we walked for five days before we could get a lorry on the way. I was young though I can feel how it was when my mother tells us how it was. We lost much time when we reached the unknown land, Kakuma Refugee Camp.

We felt a lot of pain and everything was a disaster. We had to start a new life with a single parent and the memories of our elder sister who is nowhere to be found. Life in the camp was not that simple because we didn't know anyone we could trust, and we didn't have any close relatives in the camp.

My life in Kakuma is a story to tell. My family and I have lived a life of fear. The first days in the camp were full of nightmares because of the death of my father. My worst part of living in the camp was the first time we arrived in the camp when we couldn't differentiate a good person from a bad one, making us live in fear.

But things became more comfortable after we got used to the hard life of the camp, where we can go one or two days without food.

The best part came when we started going to school, and that was when I started knowing the importance of life. I made friends in the camp that I trust.

The schools in the camp have been fair since I finished my primary school education and joined secondary school. I started my secondary school in Somali Bantu Secondary School, and then I was given a scholarship to join Morneau Shepell Secondary School for Girls. I like this school because it has made a lot of changes in my education and now I have hope for a bright future.

I am now in grade 11. I have a best friend and she is called Catherine Nyang'a. She is a polite, funny, social, caring, and loving friend. The days in school are fun because we have a laboratory and a library, and the teachers teach different subjects. They are the best teachers ever.

My career goal is to be an actress and a journalist by profession. I would like to be a writer, producer, and movie director. I also wish to help the poor, orphans, street children, and widows. I have to go to university and study more when I finish my studies so I can get a job. I hope to build my own home with my family and give birth to four children.

I look up to Will Smith, Christian Bale, and Anne Hathaway as my role models. I like the way they carry themselves and I admire the way they act in movies. But because of lack of facilities to bolster my career here in the camp, I find it hard to reach my career. Nevertheless, I have hope that one day I will fulfill my dream and it will come true no matter what comes my way.

Clare: Nyimuch is already on her way to success. She acted in a small film shot in Kakuma called Bitter Tears, where she played a girl on the verge of suicide who was saved by her mother. Nyimuch treasures this experience. For one scene, the director asked Nyimuch to cry, and she struggled initially. He asked her to think of someone she loved. Nyimuch remembered her grandmother, who had died in Kakuma, and began to cry. She used to wash her grandmother's clothes and cook for her. Her grandmother told her she liked her meals and she gave Nyimuch money to buy shoes. Although she is close to her siblings and her mother, Nyimuch held a special place in her heart for her grandmother.

Through her love for acting and movies, Nyimuch has come to possess a kind of worldliness. She strives to learn outside of simple textbooks. She loves learning about people and their stories; she uses these stories as motivation and inspiration. Also impressive is Nyimuch's desire to help others. Having experienced so much pain and struggle, she wishes to help those who are suffering.

Ethiopia is bordered by Sudan, Eritrea, and Somalia, all countries that were plagued by violent warfare in the late 1990s. Some of the conflict in Sudan in the late 1990s spilled into Ethiopia.

Four years before Nyimuch was born, in 1993, Eritrea gained independence from Ethiopia. Although this temporarily solved some problems, there were frequent border disputes and heavy tension between Eritrea and Ethiopia.

Ethiopia has a rich cultural history but also a ragged history of corruption, violence, and famine, along with military coups. Ethiopia was under Haile Selassie's rule for a long time. After sixty years as emperor, he was finally ousted in a military coup in 1974. Military general Teferi Benti became head of state, only to be killed and replaced three years later by Colonel Mengistu Haile Mariam.

Ethiopia faced two famines during the 1970s and 1980s, and during these periods hundreds of thousands of people died of starvation. The crises in Ethiopia did not end when Mengistu

fled the country in 1991; fighting continued between Ethiopia and Eritrea, and ethnic conflict was common, forcing many civilians to flee their homes for fear of persecution. Conflict continued throughout the 2000s, with bombings in Addis Ababa, Ethiopia's capital, and renewed fighting with Somalia.

While currently there is no war in Ethiopia, coup attempts are common and civilians struggle with environmental problems such as persistent droughts. There is still underlying tension between government and rebel forces, although the recent electoral victory of the Ethiopian People's Revolutionary Democratic Front has appeased many Ethiopian civilians.

Many of Ethiopia's most extreme struggles and conflicts occurred decades ago, but they have left a residue on the civilians and infrastructure of Ethiopia. Even though Nyimuch is not old enough to have experienced the rule of dictator Mengistu, she recalls that her time in Ethiopia was marked by havoc and fragility.

Although there has been much progress, it has not been enough to allow some refugees like Nyimuch to go home. The majority of Ethiopians still live below the poverty line and are illiterate. Concerns in Ethiopia today are limits to media freedom, internal and regional insecurity, and the impact of climate change.

As well, Ethiopia is currently the largest refugee-hosting country in Africa, mainly providing asylum for refugees from South Sudan, Somalia, and Eritrea. There have been massive floods in three of the new refugee camps, causing tents and shelters to collapse. The flooding has made the refugee situation in Ethiopia worse and has increased health risks for refugees and Ethiopians alike. If Nyimuch's family was to go home, it's uncertain how their life there would compare to the one they have in Kakuma.

Nyimuch is determined and eager to succeed in life. She is desperate to leave Kakuma, to be involved in film, and to help make the world a better place. I really want to see Nyimuch in a movie one day.

Democratic Republic of Congo

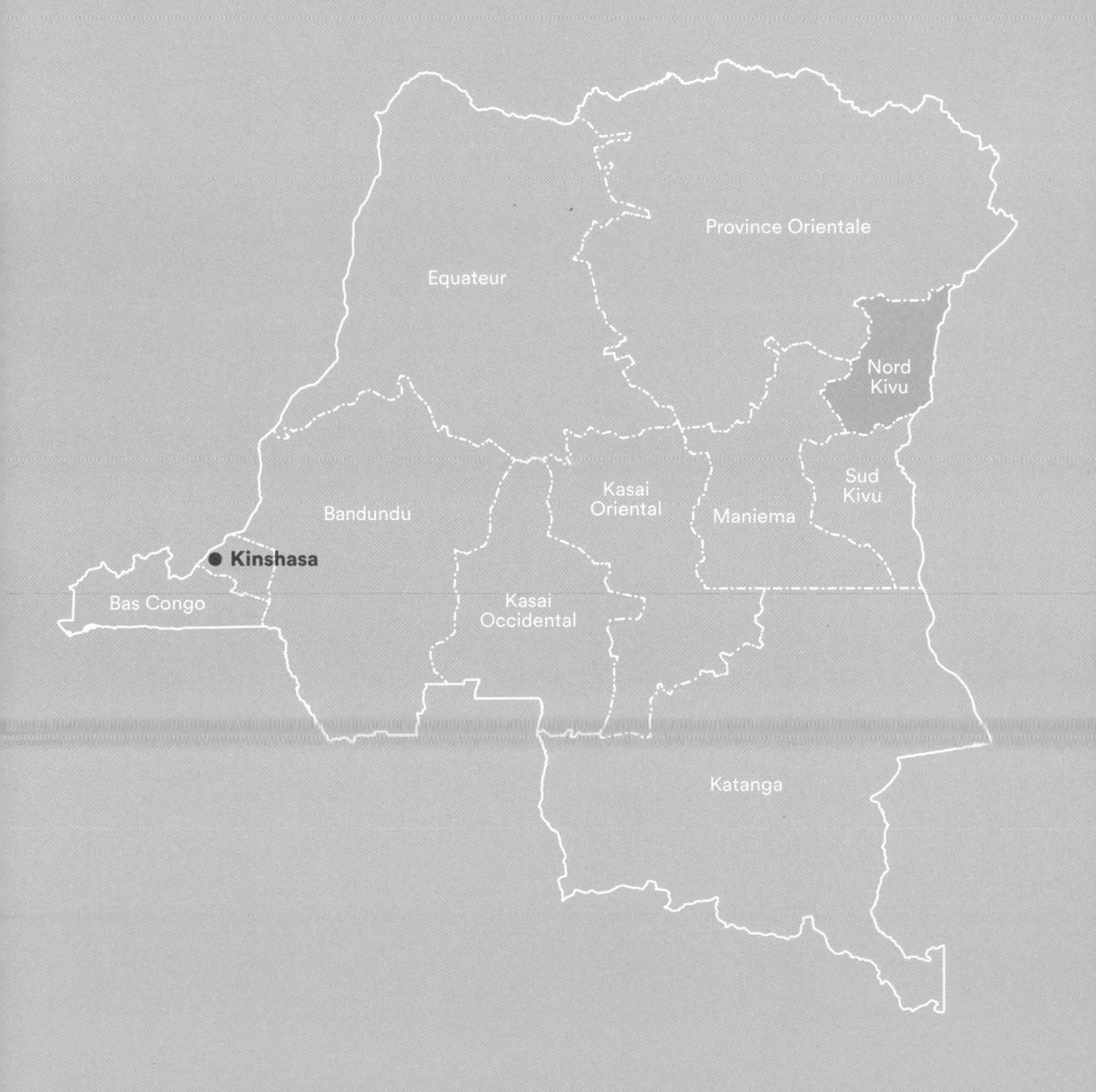

Equateur

Province Orientale

Bandundu

Nord Kivu

Kasai Oriental

Maniema

Sud Kivu

● **Kinshasa**

Bas Congo

Kasai Occidental

Katanga

Christine Bachoke

Life in Kakuma is not that good because you are not free to do what you need to do. It is like being caged birds who can only move inside the cage. On the other hand, it is good because we are still alive and we can get free education and strive for the future.

My name is Christine Bachoke, I was born in the Democratic Republic of Congo (DRC) on February 7, 1996. I was born at a hospital and my parents were present. I have a big sister (twenty-five) and a stepsister. I am the last born of my mother's womb. My family is polygamous. My father had two wives.

My biological parents passed on when I was only two years old. I have three paternal uncles and two aunts. I also have one maternal uncle, three aunts, and eight cousins. I live with my sisters, one nephew, two nieces, and my brother-in-law.

Congo is the second largest country in Africa and got her independence in 1960. My country is beautiful, having lakes such as Lake Albert. She has natural vegetation and many parks containing extraordinary animals, but I did not have a chance to live there for long.

I believe my country is very rich, but the citizens very poor. I would like that to end in the coming years. Congo has about 200 tribes; these include Kishi, Fulero, Kikongo, and Kasai. My father is from Kishi.

I lived in the Congo for a few years but because of some problems after the death of my parents, we had to go to my aunt's house in Rwanda with my mom, who is Rwandan.

The first days in the camp were mysterious, but we had to be patient. During the days that I was new to Kakuma, I was surprised that you cannot move or cook during daytime due to much dust and wind, so we waited until evening when the sun had set, or else we did it very early in the morning.

I will never forget the day I was told that I am joining a boarding school. I do not prefer living in the camp, so I will work harder and harder and pray to God so that I get out of the camp.

In the camp there is discrimination. On the other hand, living in the camp is only good when you socialize with different tribes, nationalities, and cultures. Also knowing different languages, knowing new people, and making new friendships is good.

For ours Morneau Shepell School was like a salvation for many girls in the camp and outside the camp, especially to me, because I was helpless. We were chosen because we were the top-performing or the most vulnerable girls. Classes are not difficult because everything in this world for me I think is more difficult, depending on how you take it.

In school I have a best friend from Rwanda, named Harriet. Harriet is very loving and caring. In the morning, she must make sure she knows my mood and if I am healthy. She normally encourages me that though I am an orphan, I will still make it if I work hard. Our teachers in school are friendly and caring.

Religion is important in our lives because through the regulations set by the religion, we

have the chance to fit in any society. Religion does not encourage immoralities so it helps us behave well. It also helps us know God as our creator. We practice our religion by meeting every Sunday and praising God.

As an adult, I would like to finish my education. I have two career goals: one is being an engineer and one is being a writer. I want to write books that can change the society and write scripts that can be acted by movie stars. I consider a lady called Natasha Likimani to be my role model. She is a scriptwriter in Kenya. She passed through many challenges but she never gave up. She never counted how many times she fell but only how many times she

rose; she is so inspiring.

I wish to go to a Canadian university after my secondary studies.

I wish to have children once I have finished my education and gotten a job. I wish to live in a good place, and have a car and my own compound. I really want to enjoy my life because I have never enjoyed it. I also do not want my kids to go through what I have gone through. I wish for them to be in a good place and attend a good school.

My obstacles in life are living in poverty and being parentless. Sometimes it disturbs my mind and I think that I cannot make it, but I hope I will make it and live an inspiring life.

Clare: The Democratic Republic of the Congo (DRC) is in the centre of Africa, and is bordered by Angola, Burundi, the Central African Republic, the Republic of the Congo, Rwanda, South Sudan, Tanzania, Uganda, and Zambia.

Although the DRC has very little arable land, it has long been known for its vast economic and natural resources. The country has every thing it needs to be prosperous, yet it is infamous for being an epicentre of conflict in Africa.

After a long period under Belgian rule, the DRC gained independence in 1960 and appointed a president and a prime minister.

This democracy did not last long, with government problems beginning less than six months after independence. In 1965, Joseph Mobutu replaced the government after he gained power in a coup. Mobutu held power for 32 years. His rule was corrupt and repressive. While Mobutu bought champagne and European homes, civilians under his dictatorship did not have access to basic medicines and supplies.

In 1997, the year after Christine was born, rebels captured the capital of what was Zaire,

ending Mobutu's corrupt rule and renaming the country the DRC. The civilians placed their hope in their country's new president, Laurent Kabila. Kabila was seen as a saviour for the Democratic Republic of the Congo, one who would end corruption. However, in 1998 rebels who were formerly allies of Kabila began fighting against him. This prompted what is known as Africa's World War. From 1998 to 2003 forces backed by Namibia, Zimbabwe, and Angola fought against rebels backed by Rwanda and Uganda. The war devastated the DRC, leaving an estimated six million people dead and a nonexistent government.

In 2003, the United Nation's efforts to create peace in the DRC seemed successful, as they were able to stop much of the fighting and an interim parliament was put into power. However, this fragile peace was short-lived. Rebels continue to fight back against the government and there have been many cases of rebel forces from other countries entering the Democratic Republic of the Congo.

Amid all of this fighting, civilians living in the

country have suffered from a deadly outbreak of the Ebola virus in 2007, rape epidemics, lack of health and social services, and ongoing crime. No matter who intervenes or who is in power, fighting continues, and more and more civilians suffer and die in the crossfire. Hundreds of thousands of civilians have fled the DRC, seeking asylum in neighbouring countries.

I hope Christine becomes a journalist and tells her stories as she has such a desire to learn and write. With her determination and perseverance, as well as support for education, there is no reason why she can't also be an engineer.

Background on the Refugee Crisis and Kakuma

Background on the Refugee Crisis and Kakuma

A refugee is legally defined as someone fleeing his or her country of origin due to fear of persecution for reasons of race, nationality, religion, or association with a particular social or political group and opinion.

Many refugees are the unlucky victims of political violence. When civilians are subject to conditions resulting from conflict, globalization, climate change, and human rights issues, they are forced to decide whether they will stay in their home country and risk danger or flee their country and leave behind their life. When refugees flee, many enter bordering countries in their search for asylum. Many refugees travel for miles and years in order to find any semblance of asylum, ultimately ending up in camps.

A camp is defined as any settlement where refugees are housed and aided by humanitarian and government organizations.

Refugee camps ease the distribution of protection and assistance to large groups of refugees and internally displaced people. However, camps can often feel stifling as they restrict one's ability to move freely and make important decisions for themselves. Camps can make it difficult to foster independence and self-sufficiency. Sadly, the average time spent in a refugee camp has increased from nine to twenty years—people's migration journeys are entire lifetimes for some, including several girls at Morneau Shepell Secondary School for Girls.

Largest number of people fleeing in history

According to the UNHCR today there are over 60 million forcibly displaced people worldwide. Or put another way, 1 out of every 122 people is a refugee or an internally displaced or asylum-seeking person.

This number has increased dramatically in the past several years. Since 2014, over 13 million more people are in flight. This past year, 2015, set the record for the highest annual increase in displaced people. At the moment, approximately 42,500 people are displaced daily, an unprecedented number in the post-World War II era. What is even more shocking is that approximately 51 per cent of the refugee population is made up of children under the age of eighteen, a number that has increased ten per cent in the last five years.

The main causes of these upsetting statistics are the new and continuing crises, conflicts and disasters around the world. The majority of

Global Refugees
by Country of Origin 2014

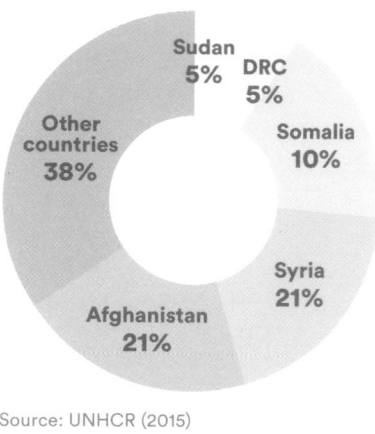

Sudan 5%
DRC 5%
Somalia 10%
Other countries 38%
Syria 21%
Afghanistan 21%

Source: UNHCR (2015)

refugees and internally displaced people originate from countries in the Middle East, Africa, as well as Europe (Ukraine), Asia, and Central America. They are forced to travel to neighbouring countries and then third or fourth countries, sometimes in dangerous or overcrowded boats, to seek asylum from persecution, extreme poverty and conflict.

The horrible war in Syria is causing a massive increase in the global refugee population, as it is responsible for creating one fourth of displaced persons globally. Many of these displaced people travel to countries such as Turkey, Pakistan, Lebanon, Ethiopia, and Kenya, which are some of the top refugee-hosting countries in the world. Some countries such as Germany are responding to the crisis by opening their doors generously, but Canada has lagged behind in the resettlement of refugees until recently. The refugee influx from Syria has become so great that countries like Hungary, Turkey, Bulgaria and Greece actually built walls in an effort to keep refugees out.

The rapid acceleration and the scale of global forced displacement is alarming and will continue if politicians do not address the roots of injustices, war, and climate change.

In addition to the huge global crisis of increasing numbers of refugees is the challenges faced by refugees who have been in exile for over five years. Over 6.4 million refugees have been residing in refugee camps for an extended period of time, some for over twenty years. This is due to the lack of long-term solutions for refugees, with the only conceivable ones being voluntary return, local integration or resettlement in third countries. Relocation options for refugees are limited because there are not enough host countries willing to fully accept refugees.

Many countries are passive observers or do not take the number of refugees they can take or have historically taken. So many places around the world, like North America, Europe and some Gulf states, are dedicating too little attention to this crisis, believing that it is not their problem. This is increasingly common in wealthy countries, which only host 14 per cent of the world's refugees. The massive increases in refugee populations have escalated border tension and hostility between many countries, making it more difficult for refugees to seek asylum. Furthermore, refugees are increasingly viewed as job-seekers and terrorists, making

Major Refugee-hosting Countries at the End of 2014

Source: UNCHR (December 2014)

them even more unwelcome in wealthy nations. Fewer countries are concerned with protecting refugees or preventing refugee movement and are instead attempting to determine how to keep asylum-seekers outside their borders, sometimes resorting to such tactics as building fences and implementing new policies of exclusion.

If the number of refugees continues to rise at its current rate, humanitarian organizations and refugee-hosting countries will be in further crisis; they are already overwhelmed and under-funded. The numbers of refugees and internally displaced people will continue to increase due to natural disasters and climate change, but the conflict and crises in many countries that drive

the refugee crisis can be prevented. It is not realistic to assume that even the most socially advanced countries will be able to host every refugee that passes their way, as their financial budgets and land mass may not allow it. If the world does not share the job of helping those who have been forcibly displaced, those people will have nowhere to go.

I hope these countries will step up and open their doors to more refugees. These refugees are not here to take jobs—they are fleeing persecution, simply hoping to find a country where they will be welcomed and accepted for who they are and what they believe in.

Girls' Education in Conflict Zones and Refugee Contexts

In conflict zones, 10 million girls are not in school.

Half of all out-of-school children live in conflict-affected countries.

One in four of refugee children is estimated to be in secondary school, of those out of school the majority are girls.

1%

Just one per cent of young refugees are enrolled in tertiary education.

In total more than 60 million girls are out of school today.

School Enrollment in Kakuma Refugee Camp
(of eligible students)

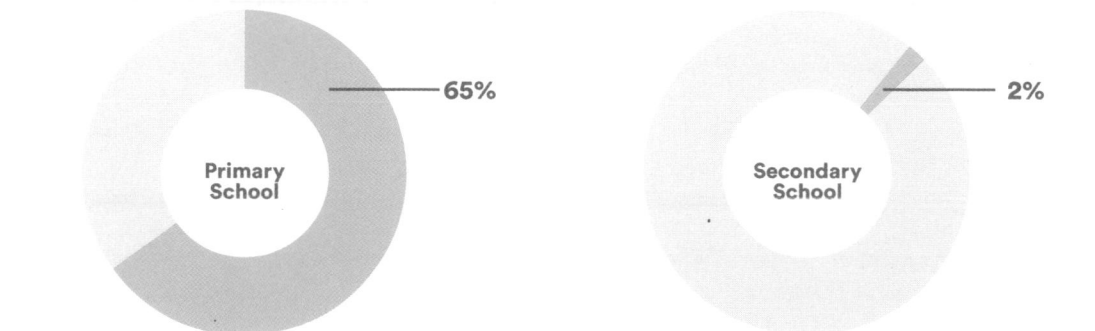

Primary School — 65%

Secondary School — 2%

Top sources: Women's Refugee Commission, UNESCO, UNCHR, UNCHR, OHCHR; Bottom: UNHCR (2015)

The Havergal/Kakuma Partnership

Lois Rowe, Vice Principal, Havergal College

On the surface, the girls who attend Havergal College in Toronto, Canada, and the girls who attend the Morneau Shepell Secondary School for Girls in the Kakuma Refugee Camp, Kenya, have little in common apart from gender. And then, through letters and notes, they have met. Through words on paper, students have discovered that they are alike in deep and meaningful ways. Discovering that a girl who is living a very different life nearly 12,000 kilometres away shares your value for education, your willingness to strive toward realizing your own capability, and your desire to make a positive difference in the world, somehow makes the world a little bit smaller and speaks to the power of a global community.

Havergal College is proud to support the Kakuma Toronto Girls Education Partnership. As a school whose mission revolves around *Preparing Young Women to Make a Difference,* Havergal believes in developing the distinct and powerful voices of girls as change agents in the world. Situated in the multicultural city of Toronto and home to boarding school students whose homes are in countries across the globe, students at Havergal experience the strength that comes from hearing and understanding different perspectives. Moreover, by attending a school that promotes and honours girls as learners and leaders, Havergal students recognize that they have a crucial role to play and a responsibility to contribute to the world. This is the perspective that travels with the letters and notes from the Havergal students to the girls of Kakuma. And, knowing there are other girls in the world who are cheering them on can only strengthen the Kakuma girls' resolve to overcome the barriers they face in order to pursue an education and to confidently chart their own course.

The Kakuma Toronto Girls Education Partnership has expanded the communities for both schools. More importantly, this partnership has created solid bonds of friendship and understanding between the girls at Havergal and girls in the Kakuma Refugee Camp. By opening up both their worlds to each other, this partnership has made the hopes and dreams of these girls a reality firmly within their grasps.

Why Investing in Girls' Education Delivers Results

When we fail to invest in girls' education:
millions of girls and women are locked out of opportunities

Globally, 62 million children
are not in primary school.
More than half are girls[1]

There are 781 million
illiterate adults worldwide.
2 of 3 are women[1]

When we successfully invest in girls' education:

Life expectancy increases

Women's education
has prevented 4 million child
deaths in the past 40 years[2]

Women earn more

One additional school year
can increase a woman's
earnings by 10 to 20 per cent[3]

Economies prosper

Could boost agricultural
output in sub-Saharan
Africa by 25 per cent[4]

A child whose mother
can read is 50 per cent more
likely to live past age 5[3]

A one per cent increase in
the number of women with a
secondary education raises
a nation's annual per capita economic growth by 0.3 per cent[5]

Sources: Global Partnership for Education. 1. UNESCO Institute for Statistics. 2. UNGEI Engendering Empowerment Report, 2012.
3. UNESCO Education for all Global Monitoring Report, 2011. 4. IFPRI Women Still Key to Food and Nutrition Security Paper, 2005.
5. World Bank "Measuring the Economic Gain of Investing in Girls," 2011.

Windle Trust

"What girls at Morneau Shepell Secondary School for Girls need now is scholarship funding. Windle Trust chooses girls based on their scores and available scholarship opportunities, but if others provided the funding it would be great. It gets cold at night and some girls do not have enough sweaters. They need sweaters. Books are needed but not all book donations are appropriate. It's really important to find out what books schools need before sending books."

—Raphael Sungu, Program Manager

Windle Trust Kenya helps implement Morneau Shepell Secondary School for Girls. It's a non-governmental organization in Kenya and a member of Windle Trust International Federation. Windle Trust Kenya started in 1977 to assist refugees and Kenyans in need. It focuses on educational scholarships for students in the camp and in the host community.

There are four secondary schools in Kakuma including Morneau Shepell Secondary School for Girls. (MSSSG). Top-performing girls who get above 300 are placed at MSSSG. Windle Trust wants this school to be a centre for excellence; a place for girls to excel. While the Trust is not yet giving scholarships to students (the first group of girls are not in their graduating year at MSSSG) they aim to make the school impactful and attractive.

The long-term goal is to have a scholarship plan for MSSSG. Next year the first group graduates, so the girls who don't get WUSC scholarships will need other scholarships. Windle Trust wishes to help see the girls through school and to track the girls at all secondary schools, including those who don't get scholarships.

MSSSG has a dedicated principal and teaching staff. Windle Trust aims to increase the number of female teachers at the school. There are two teachers living at the school now.

In all Kakuma schools Windle Trust addresses barriers girls face when it comes to receiving education (protection, cultural and economic barriers) and aims to help girls access education, monitor their progress, and assist them to complete the school cycle.

Tools for success for girls' education, Kakuma Refugee Camp Inspired by Windle Trust (WT)

Solar lamps
Usually girls do chores at night and by the time they are done it is dark, so these lamps are a valuable study tool.

Uniforms
When families can't afford uniforms, their girls can't go to school. WT has found if the uniforms are in bad shape or worn, some girls won't attend school.

Teaching and learning materials
Additional teachers help reduce the teacher/pupil ratio; additional classrooms and remedial classes give girls a better chance to succeed.

Girls' and Boys' Clubs
These clubs are important for building youth leadership and providing activities to enhance girls' and boys' education.

Girl-friendly toilets
WT helps school managers think about privacy and ensuring that there is an adequate number of toilets for girls. For cultural reasons often girls cannot be seen entering toilets so making screens and planning locations matters.

Small Funds
Schools send proposals to WT who supports in-kind projects e.g., a school tree-planting environmental initiative.

Scholarships for university and pre-university courses
Ninety-five students from Kakuma are now on scholarships through Windle Trust. The scholarships are for students who performed well in various schools. Girls with protection challenges also get scholarships.

Sanitary products
The girls need sanitary products so they can attend school.

Peace Club
Students from different countries, tribes and cultures meet and exchange ideas so the message about peace gets out.

Computers and ICT
WT piloted networked schools in Dadaab and now has a green light for a pilot school in Kakuma with computers and an instant network with Safaricom.

Life in Kakuma Refugee Camp

Although some in the Western world may view refugee camps as a good solution for refugee crises, they are not as ideal as they seem. Refugee camps, although often slightly better than the countries the refugees originate from, can also be hopeless places, as they often lack a feeling of permanence. Refugees in camps are unable to move around freely and work. Many refugee camps also have drawbacks that include overcrowding, disease, and insufficient resources.

Food

The minimum WFP/UNHCR standard for food is 2100 calories per person daily; Kakuma attempts to adhere to this standard. However, there are often food shortages due to budget cuts, so many refugees find that they do not have enough to eat. While organizations like WFP and UNHCR do their best to provide refugees with the calories they need, they are often not able to accommodate the specific foods that many of the refugees are used to eating. This forces refugees to use whatever money they have to buy the foods that they are culturally accustomed to, in order to foster a sense of normalcy. Many refugees also sell their food in order to obtain money for other needs and luxuries.

Aid organizations such as the World Food Program in the past have handed out ration cards with which refugees can obtain food. Recently, a new cash transfer option has been introduced into Kakuma Refugee Camp. Cash is sent through a mobile phone and can be redeemed for food, allowing refugees to choose what food they want to buy instead of having others choose for them. This cash transfer process also increases business between refugees and shopkeepers, fostering an economic community in the camp while also minimizing the risk of theft. One issue with the new cash transfer option is that not everyone in the camp has access to a mobile phone, leaving some refugees to depend on the old process of receiving rations while others get to choose their food. Some refugees also prefer the old option, and there is worry that the new system may cause food prices to surge.

Okra, also known as "Lady Fingers," was introduced by farmers in the region after maize crops were devastated by disease in 2007. Vendors also sell kale in the market. Some good things grow here, but Kakuma is largely inhospitable for the 100,000+ local population because of constant drought and land unsuitable for most agriculture.

Girls collecting water near the Lodwar-Lokichogio road. This task is one of many that girls are responsible for. Seven new boreholes have been dug recently so water is more plentiful, but not yet enough per person according to UNHCR's standards. Locals and refugees are hopeful that they will soon have access to more water sources.

A boy in the camp. In 2016 the new refugee arrivals in Kakuma are mainly women and children, a majority of whom are boys. Kakuma registered 2,360 unaccompanied minors by February 2016. The Reception Centre reports that of the new arrivals in Kakuma since 2014, many are children including boys fleeing South Sudan to avoid military recruitment.

Water

The lack of water poses problems in Kakuma. The minimum standard per capita distribution of water should be at least 20 litres according to UNHCR. In Kakuma, it is 15 litres, only three-fourths of the required amount. Although there are seventeen operational water boreholes in Kakuma, these can still be a long distance from certain places in the camp, meaning that refugees sometimes have to walk long distances for their water. Two large aquifers of water in Turkana County were discovered by satellite technology in 2013. Hopefully all who need it will be able to access this new water if it is made available. Climate change is a challenge for everyone everywhere, so equitable access to precious resources such as water will be essential.

Shelter

Several organizations are attempting to provide more permanent housing in Kakuma. Less than 50 per cent of dwellings in Kakuma currently qualify as adequate shelter, so these organizations have a lot of work ahead of them. A large portion of the population of Kakuma lives in temporary shelters or badly constructed semi-permanent shelters. Many households are in need of proper roofing and this need only increases with rain and flooding. The weather conditions in Kakuma can cause the weaker shelters to collapse and wash away in floods, forcing refugees to rebuild their homes.

Sanitation

Sanitation continues to be an issue in Kakuma Refugee Camp. There are not enough latrines to provide the entire population with an adequate number of toilets. At the moment, 45 per cent of houses in the camp share latrines, with an average of one latrine for every fifteen people.

This ratio is much larger in schools—so large, in fact, that the lack of sufficient latrines in schools can deter students from attending, particularly girls.

Sanitation is also affected by the weather in the camp. When there is flooding, there is an increased chance of waterborne diseases and bacteria spreading throughout the camp. Garbage can also be carried by the water, and can end up flooding into refugee shelters.

Violence

Refugee camps can be dangerous, with abundant violence and conflict. Conflicts that originated in other countries often follow refugees to refugee camps, causing conflicts to continue in the camps. Furthermore, with the limited activities available in the camps, people have few outlets for their frustration and boredom, causing them to turn to violence. Historically Kakuma has been impacted by violence between exiles of the same nationality. However, in 2014 eight people in Kakuma were killed in interethnic violence.

Kakuma Refugee Camp, although viewed as a safe haven for citizens fleeing dangerous situations, is not always as safe as it is perceived.

This can destroy the sense of safety from persecution that the majority of refugees hope to find in refugee camps. For example, there has been tension between many people of the Dinka and Nuer tribes living in Kakuma Refugee Camp. In November 2014, violence erupted between the Dinka and Nuer tribes after an alleged rape of a ten-year-old refugee child. Refugees of one tribe often blame refugees from the other tribe for the destruction of peace in South Sudan, effectively continuing the current conflict occurring in South Sudan in the refugee camp.

Problems can be triggered when someone

A home in Kakuma refugee camp. Like many of the older dwellings without tin roofs, its walls include reinforced plastic marked with the UNHCR label. This is a symbol of shelter, but paradoxically, also a marker of the loss of home.

A tailor in one of Kakuma's many markets. Traders in the market are from both the local population and the refugee population. Some Turkana in remote Kakuma say that refugees get more opportunities than they, the local population, do, but for all there are few economic opportunities.

Like clockwork, as the sun lowers in the sky, young people get out their balls and play. Former Kakuma refugee and professional footballer Awer Mabil (FC Midtjylland) with others started Barefoot to Boots, "an Australian initiative to provide football boots, shirts and balls to refugees, [to] provide joy and improve health and safety for those living in refugee camps.

is already frustrated with the lack of resources, opportunity and freedom that they have. Although organizations like UNHCR and WFP provide refugees with packages of essentials every month, the refugees are often discontent with these packages as they do not contain their specific cultural food or items they feel they need. This frustration can easily turn into anger, which some refugees release in ways that jeopardize the safety of people in the camp.

There is also a fear of the local people that live near Kakuma Refugee Camp, particularly the Turkana people. The Turkana often feel that the refugees are receiving support from the Kenyan government that they should be receiving. There have been reports of Turkana people raiding the camp for supplies and attacking refugees. Likewise, some Turkana feel their wellbeing is threatened by the camp.

Gender-based Violence and Concerns for Girls in Refugee Camps

Girls and women are extremely vulnerable in the camps. In order to get water, some women and girls have to walk long distances from their homes, making them easy to attack. They are susceptible to rape, domestic violence, genital mutilation, trafficking, and abduction. These types of gender-based violence can contribute to the destruction of a woman's identity and can create paralyzing insecurity, fear, and both physical and psychosocial health problems.

For girls attending day schools, the journey to school is more perilous than it is for male students. In addition to the challenges caused by weather and dangerous animals such as poisonous snakes, girl students live in fear of sexual assault and abduction. It is not uncommon for a girl to get assaulted on her walk to school, especially if she is walking alone.

In many cultures, including Somali and Sudanese cultures, girls are often forced into getting married and having children at increasingly young ages. Many parents cannot envision the results of schooling, instead believing they will gain more from marrying off their daughters for a price. Girls are also expected to do all of the housework, leaving no time for them to study or get an education.

In Kakuma Refugee Camp, many nonprofit organizations try to encourage parents to educate their daughters. Some organizations provide scholarships and assistance for female students, but there are not enough to allow every girl and boy to receive higher education.

Some women and girls in refugee camps are also trafficked, forced to turn to prostitution in order to earn money, or they are forced to trade sex for goods. When a girl's family has no means of income, sometimes the girl is made to feel that her body is the only means of currency she has.

At the moment, there are few safe havens for women in the camp and few centres for survivors of gender-based violence in Kakuma, other than two operated by Jesuit Refugee Service. The protection areas are isolated from the rest of the camp and are extremely limited.

Organizations such as UNHCR are actively trying to improve the lives of women in Kakuma. Although gender can typically deny women and girls the ability to make important decisions, female refugees can hold their own food cards or receive direct cash transfers, so they no longer have to rely on men for their food and survival. This helps empower women and girls and sends a message that women and men can be equal in the refugee camp.

Kakuma 4 is the newest of of the refugee camp sectors, built largely to house the large, new influx of people fleeing conflict in South Sudan. This is one of the camp's phone charging stations. Cellular phones give the refugees some autonomy as having a phone means being able to receive mobile cash transfers and connect to the world outside.

Kakuma Secondary School. The school compound consists of several single-storey classrooms. One classroom has a gaping hole in the wall because resources are not available to make repairs. Classrooms are packed, teaching materials are poor, but there are students in their white uniform tops, a majority boys, who are lucky to be in class.

Sign in Kakuma 4: "Are you aware of Prevention of Sexual Exploitation & Abuse?" Structural violence and sexual and gender violence against women and girls, as well as boys and men (though under-reported), is a problem in Kakuma as it is in other refugee and non-refugee situations.

Notes from Kakuma
Carol Devine to Clare Morneau

July 13, 2015

Dear Clare,

Greetings from Kakuma!

I didn't expect such wind when we stepped off the World Food Programme plane onto Turkana country land. It was barely 9:00 am and the sun was hot.

From the plane we had seen a sea of humanity moving among tin-roofed houses, houses made of plastic, and mud-brick homes surrounded by reddish-brown soil. Jjumba and I had met before sunrise at Nairobi's Wilson Airport to catch this flight. He'd arrived the night before from Kampala with his photo gear.

Here hundreds of thousands of refugees live amidst the host population, largely of Kenya's Turkana and Pokot ethnic groups.

This feels like a dusty, forgotten part of the world. Well, not totally forgotten, thank goodness.

Kakuma means 'nowhere' in Kiswahili. Not only are the local people some of Kenya's poorest citizens but few refugees in this overcrowded camp have the chance to return home or resettle elsewhere.

At the airstrip to greet us were Mohamud and Catherine from the UNHCR. Mohamud is Kakuma's Education Officer, a Kenyan Somali and former high school teacher in Dadaab's massive refugee camp on the other side of Kenya. Catherine is Kenyan, a public information officer. What kind and generous people they are.

I wish you'd seen the faces of the young women who came into the classroom to meet Jjumba and me. Thank you for sending me here to be your eyes and ears.

Beautiful, shy and keen girls smiled at us. They looked lovely in crisp robin's egg blue uniforms. I'm putting names to faces from the profiles the girls had written and sent you. Christine, Lula, Nhial. Who would know the horror most of them or their parents had faced at some point, the majority fleeing violent situations, or in the case of quiet Amach, only knowing this camp her entire life?

Lula was the first to ask questions. She's thoughtful, intensely curious and has a kind of formality.

"I will do my level best at school," Lula promised. She said how life-changing and hopeful the school is.

With an insatiable thirst the girls want to know about the world. I told them to ask me any questions since I would be asking them many.

Where have you been in the world?

How does this camp compare to other refugee camps?

When were you most scared?

What is university like?

What does a school look like in Canada?

What do your children want to be when they grow up?

These young women are incredible. They personify dignity and resilience. I worry a bit about them, but they are in a place of hope. This school is a tangible gift and support to girls who seem to be the most vulnerable and the bravest girls in the world all at once.

More tomorrow,
Carol

The girls tell us their friends are an important part of their support system. Spend any time at the school and you see this. Several girls are orphans or heads of households because their parents are back home. The school is also an oasis and opportunity for the small number of local Kenyan girls who attend.

"Safe Haven" sign at the United Nations High Commissioner for Refugees building in Kakuma. This appears to be a mustering station in case of emergencies: a safe haven within a safe haven.

Midday lesson at MSSSG. The girls start early and have a break in the afternoon when the sun is at its hottest.

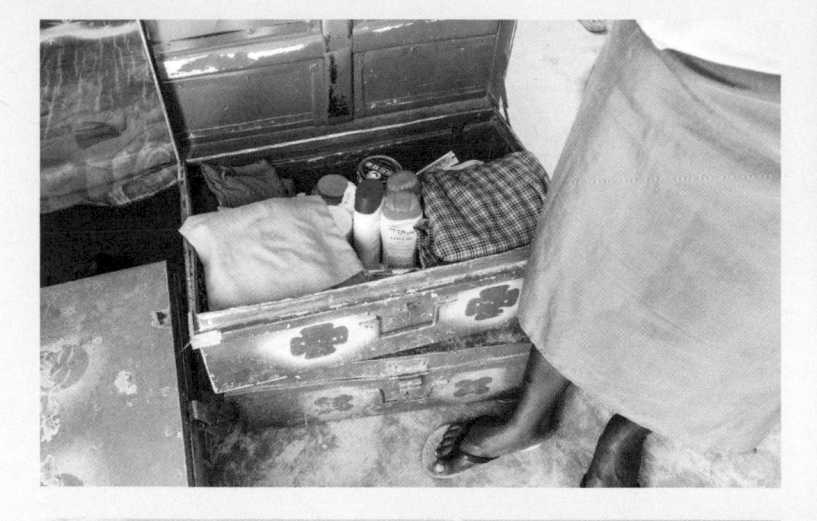

This girl in her dorm shows me her "Life in a Box," her personal trunk. How precious must the few possessions they have with them at the school be.

Before sunset girls are busy at the outdoor water taps washing themselves and their clothes. This day the water tank broke and the girls were extremely patient and good-natured despite their thirst and inability to clean themselves. While there are cooks at MSSSG to make their meals, the girls do their own chores and self-care.

Girls go to their dorms during the afternoon break when the sun peaks. Kenya is on the equator so there is no summer or winter, only the rains. These girls hamming it up remind me of teenage girls in Toronto.

July 14, 2015
Dear Clare,
In the morning we arrived at the school at sunrise. The girls were milling about, some were shining their shoes.

Christine, pulling on her bright white socks, told me she rose at 4:30 am, had prayers at 5:00 am, ate breakfast then started chores. Next she'd do physics homework.

I'm moved by Christine because I worked in Rwanda and the Congo (then Zaire) at the time she would have been born there after the Rwandan genocide and into the ensuing violence.

Christine's an orphan. On Visitor's Day she said she feels sad and worthless. Christine was going to let herself be forced into marriage to end her destitution when the MSSSG opportunity came. She's smart, kind, and confident though humble, and has a cheeky sweet smile. I can't imagine being on the move and parentless from age two with extended family who can't support you. She has one cousin here— that fact, and school, are her solace.

The girls are busy and disciplined with studying as well as doing school chores.

I loved visiting the dorms. A flurry of voices and activity. The house mother Veronica had a pretend cranky look on her face but she seems full of humour and takes good care of the girls. She saw me and egged the girls on by saying, "Keep sweeping!" Then she winked at me.

The camaraderie of the girls, despite the lack of personal space, is at first surprising, then you know this place is a haven and they appreciate it. I asked one girl how she liked living with all these girls and she replied, "It's fine— I have many sisters at home."

Esther, a politically astute girl from South Sudan who loves soccer, joked with me that I could help them and stay over in the dorm.

I was lucky to sit in on a social studies class about population growth. The girls were deeply focused. The teachers seem dedicated and supportive here.

What you and Morneau Shepell and Havergal are doing is meaningful and impactful.

Carol

P.S. Today I saw this quote in an article *Riding on the back of a tortoise* by Ethiopian author Abebe Feyissa Demo.

> "There are only bodies in Kakuma. Everyone's souls are traveling; they have gone for resettlement, completed interrupted college studies, in the world of daydreams."

Demo has lived in Kakuma camp since 1993, he fled in 1991 during his studies at University of Addis Ababa, Ethiopia when student leaders were being persecuted.

July 15, 2015
Jambo again Clare,
I've visited the school three days in a row, and I'm delighted that it exists and that I have had the honour of meeting these girls.

We spoke to and photographed more girls and watched classes in action. We toured the school library. On shelves were multicoloured English text books. I know you girls in Toronto sent those precious books here—what a lovely connection to make between young women across the globe.

I was struck to see the similarities you told me you and your peers had discovered with these girls. They are eager for the future but are uncertain about what's next. They are curious and intelligent, and it makes me believe in the promise of the future knowing you girls are helping to shape it.

These girls realize they are lucky compared to girls in Kakuma who cannot attend school, or girls in their home countries, just as you and your friends realize you're lucky in Canada.

The friendships you and your fellow students are building are cherished. The girls told me, "We love the letter-writing with the girls in Canada. We want our story told, this book project makes us excited."

Two things I'll not soon forget:

The girls at 3:30 pm in the heat taking a siesta. The bustling dorms were like a scene from the *Madeline* book series, set in a fictional girls boarding school in Paris. We're not in France but in Kenya, some 90 km from the border of South Sudan, the protracted, violent civil war many of the girls living here fled.

In the dorm girls were in little groups chatting, others were reading or resting.

Below the dorm beds were colourful rectangular trunks holding the girls few possessions. Hanging above the beds in daytime were mosquito nets neatly wrapped in a ball like cocoons.

Another thing I'll remember was that at sunset the girls walked to their classrooms to do homework. The classrooms are called Violet and Purple. The heat and dryness was still palpable. I passed a group of girls, one girl was eating an orange. She offered me a slice. I gratefully accepted and gave a thumbs up. The girls laughed. There was a problem with the water tank that day and the girls were so patient. They know the value of each drop of water.

When I went to bed I could hear crickets chirping outside. I was thinking of the girls in their dorms, wondering what they think of late at night. Some must worry, and hopefully, some must have dreams that will come true.

Here the girls say they feel safe. They receive quality education. Their home life pressures surely remain but they are given this precious and nurturing space to learn. I can't wait for you to visit the girls.

Warm (really warm) regards,
Carol

July 16, 2015
Dear Clare,
This morning the girls gathered in the building in the middle of the schoolground that serves as the auditorium, teaching, and prayer space. The headmistress announced that they would remount some of the cultural show they'd recently performed. The girls cheered.

When we returned later for the show after visiting the Reception Centre, the students had transformed themselves.

Esther was in a soccer uniform with gelled hair, and a girl I hadn't yet met was in traditional Turkana clothing, a brown, beaded shift dress. The clothing and outfits were remarkable, multicoloured intricate dresses and two-piece numbers.

They did a fashion show to contemporary music you also know: such as Beyoncé. The audience—girls and teachers and Mohamud and Cathy from the UNHCR—went wild with applause. Then the girls did cultural dances and songs. You'd have adored it.

What I loved most was when Kenyan and Somali girls alongside South Sudanese girls performed a traditional dance from South Sudan. Only in Kakuma!

The girls were wearing each other's traditional clothes and had learned each other's music and stories—although they are from several different countries, and have different ethnicities and religions, they co-exist peacefully.

Three girls did a skit about a wise community woman warning girls about a lecherous man and the importance of AIDS awareness and protecting themselves from abuse. They did not say it but I know the number one killer of adolescent girls in Africa is HIV/AIDS.

While the show was inspirational the play reminded me that girls are made vulnerable, and they face significant inequity and barriers.

We get a small window into life here. The land is parched and inhospitable. The markets are full of goods from cell phones to clothing to vegetables but I'm not sure how much people can afford to buy. The girls fear the river area because of reports of rape there. Ethnic tensions remain here.

Christine's words swirl in my head. She said being in Kakuma is like being a caged bird, but on the other hand, she is alive, studying and striving for the future.

I also think about what John who runs the Reception Centre said. There arriving refugees are registered, receive health checks, and are provided with basic goods. To the girls the centre is a bittersweet place: They have found some kind of safety, but now they have to begin again.

I asked John the best thing about his job. He replied, "It gives me courage. I meet people of many nationalities. I am motivated."

I am similarly motivated.

And I know the host countries and refugee agencies have colossal challenges ahead with so much of humanity on the move, fleeing outrageous violence, poverty and disasters—many caused by us humans.

As we were saying goodbye the light was sharp and the girls were animated. Perhaps because we were leaving and because they weren't in their uniforms there was less formality. Their questions were even more rapid fire than they had been on the first day.

I won't forget the faces or voices of the ten girls I interviewed, and the others I met along the way: Fardosa, Rita, Zahira, Nyimuch, Jennifer, Bella, Hawah, Esther and Sarah.

I think of Amach with her intense eyes and gorgeous smile, saying she wants one day to be a citizen.

Clare, I can't wait to tell you more. I'm happy to know you, the Kakuma and Canadian girls will share your stories.

See you soon,
Carol

Dear friend

Dear Friend

A big part of the Kakuma Toronto Girls Education Partnership is the letters sent between Havergal College in Toronto and the Morneau Shepell Secondary School for Girls in Kakuma.

These letters have allowed the girls on either end of the partnership to get to know their partners and learn a little bit about what life is like on the other side of the world. The following letters cannot fully capture the connection between the girls, but they are a small sample to illustrate the blossoming friendships in Kakuma and Canada.

—*Clare Morneau*

JANUARY 2015

Hey there Chelsea!
  I am Nyamuch! Happy New year to you.
I am in form three (3) this year at Morneau Shepell Girls
Secondary School with girls from different nationalities making
the school awesome and cool.

  It's soo cool to know you Chelsea and thank you for the
letter that you have written to me. I love many things and purple
is my favourite colour. I love playing volleyball, listening to music,
acting, singing, reading novels, watching movies, making fun and cracking
jokes. I also love being social. I am the second lastborn in our
family and I have three sisters. I too love laughing and staying
happy and keeping a smile on my ally's face is what I like most.
My birthday is on 20th November.. You asked for a joke but try
this tongue twister first "The big block broke the bleak braker"
Do it a little bit faster.

  There are soo many things that we are going to learn from
each's other. As long as this letters are going to keep us moving
you will get to know more about me. There is alot of stories
like for the blind rabit and the blind snake where the blind
snake shake told his blind friend to describe which animal it was.
Then the rabit told the snake that, "you are long, slimy and you
dont have eyes so you must be a Carrot!!!"
Hey Chelsea would you mind if I teach you swahili language?
STAY TUNE CHELSEA!
WORK HARD ALWAYS IN YOUR STUDIES.
REMEMBER THAT IT IS NOT OVER UNTIL IT IS OVER!!!
      BEST LUCK ALWAYS
NICE PAL

CHELSEA   FROM
                      NYAMUCH CHUOL.

Hey Nyamuch,   March 2015

Thank you for writing back to me! Your letter made me
so happy! How are you? :)

Hey! We have so many similar interests! I wish we could
play volleyball together! I love singing, too, I'm in my
school's choir! ☺ Girl, I like being funny as well, it feels
so good to make other people laugh, am I right? You seem
like such a happy and optimistic person, Nyamuch. And woah,
you must have a big family, do you ever wish for a brother?
Sometimes I wish I had a sister. And oh my goodness,
I tried it and I always messed up on the last word. And
hey, that reminds me of a poetic device that I learned
in English class. It's called alliteration, when you use
words starting with the same sound to enhance the
poem; however, alliterations aren't intense tongue
twisters! It's like: My love is _lifting_ like a _lullaby_. ☺

And of course! Tell me any, every story! I will try my best,
too, as well! Today I was dying of laughter when my
friend was trying to sit on a couch - Instead, she
missed the seat and silently fell on the floor! The
couch deceived her! ☺

One thing you should know about me is that I never
get enough sleep. ☹ I always (well, not exactly always)
stay up late doing homework or studying or procrast-
inating. And what's worse is that I have to wake up
super early to get to school on time! If anything,
napping or sleeping for me is so relaxing + essential!
How about you? What times does your school start
and finish? Havergal starts at 8:20 am and
dismisses at 3:30 pm, or 2:40pm on Wednesdays.

                                                       mae☺

And yeah, sure, I'd love to learn another language!
Let's make a deal! If you teach me swahili,
then I will teach you French?

Okay, well, here are a few words ~and phrases in French.

I wish
I could
teach you
the
pronunciation!

- Bonjour/Salut = Hello ("bonjour" literally means good day)
- Comment ça va? = How are you?
- Je t'aime. = I love you.
- Tu es mon amie = You are my friend.
- L'école = School
- Au Revoir* = Goodbye (literally means see you again)
- Bon Fête! = Happy Birthday
- J'aime rire. = I like to laugh.

Wouldn't it be cool to use Swahili/French
in our letters! I think so!!!

Anyways, I have to end my letter from here, because I
actually got to go to bed! Also, I'm really, truly
sorry that I haven't been coming to the
Skype calls! Please understand that I live far away
from the school and the calls are early in the morning.
Plus, you know me! I'm barely getting enough sleep, haha!
But Clare Morneau says that he will have them more
often, so hopefully I can come one day and see you!
It'd be so nice! I'm really sorry though, I feel bad!
Until next time, alright?

* WORK HARD AS WELL, GIRLY

Au Revoir,*

Chelsea

PS) You're so cute w/ the
inspirational messages,
thank you Nyamuch!

STAY HAPPY You're so thoughtful
and such a great
drawer

113

22nd - Jan. 2015

Hi Zoe,

My name is ANIGE. I'm 16 years old. At the moment I am so excited because of your letter of friendship that you wrote to me. On the other hand, I'm very sorry about your "PET CAT" who passed away, hoping that God will give you another beloved cat.

I live in Kakuma with my brother Aballa who is 19 years old. He is a primary school teacher. I learn at Morneau Shepell Girls Boarding Secondary School. I have two friend; Nania and Kaka. We share everything: Reading, playing and eating. When we are together all goes on well.

At school, I learn Business Studies, Geography, English and Religious. My hobbies are playing Netball and Debating. Debating aids me in improving my language.

I may say most of my entire life I didn't stay with my parents and other siblings. This is because I would like to find myself a favourable environment for learning.

Anyway I'm so excited about our friendship hoping and trusting that my wishes will be fulfiled. Thus I hope to visit canada and enjoy the life their. Zoe, I wish you all the best as I appreciate nuving a friend across the globe. Enjoy your studies as you plan to visit Africa please.

Thank you,
Anige Hashim

January 22nd 2015.

Hi Anna,

My name is Irene Mukasa. I am a Rwandese. I was born on 20th October 1999. I have 2 sisters and 2 brothers. I live with my parents here in Kakuma, Kenya. I am is Morneau Shepell secondary school. I am in form two. I have a rabbit pet called Belio which is white in colour. How Old are you? Do you have siblings and a pet?

My hobbies are dancing, listening to pop music, reading novels and magazines, playing basketball and I like badminton although I have never tried it but I always watch it on television. Will you teach me badminton?

My favourite subjects in school are Mathematics, English, Biology and History. My deskmate is Fouzia and she is a somalia. In vision 2025 I would like to be a lawyer or a Journalist. What do you want to be in future?

The temperature and life here is not easy but we have to cope with it. What about the temperature in Canada? I have hope that one day I will come to Canada for further studies. I hope you will welcome me warmly? I'm really looking forward to see the album that you told me. Keep in touch dear. Bye.

Your Penpal,
Irene.

Happy moments
Ha! Ha! Ha!

Hello Ashley Romundt,   22nd / 1 / 2014

My name is Alek Tabitha. I am 15 years old and I learn in Morneau Shepell secondary school in kakuma, Kenya. Am in grade 10.

I am really excited to get to know you through your letter. Together we can grow and create happy moments.

I am the oldest child in my family. I have 2 brothers and two sisters. I am a sudanese. Am living with my mum and siblings and my father is living far away from us. I normally miss him but I have no choice.

My hobbies are visiting new places and watching movies. I love my friends most because we chat alot and make fun during our leisure time hence in happiness. My best friend is called Angeth.

My subjects that I like most are English, Business and physics because in future I wish to work as an engineer or accoundant.

Pass my greetings to your parents and I hope we will interact more through letter writing as we share our challenges as girls.

                                        From your friend,
                                        Alek Tabitha.

Happy moments
Ha! Ha! Ha!

January, 22nd, 2015

Hi Emma,

My name is Adut Dau. I am from South Sudan and I am 16 years old. I live in kakuma with my family. I have three brothers and four sisters. Our lastborn is called Sarah. We have a cat pet called Nyadeng. I am in form two at Morneau Shepell Girls Secondary School.

I love playing netball and reading magazines, newspapers and even storybooks during my free time at school. We are taught eleven subjects in school. What about your school? My favourite classes are Biology, Chemistry and History. I would like to be a surgeon or a doctor in future. What would you like to be in future?

Life in kakuma is quite hard, the temperatures are harsh but we are used to them. How are temperatures over there? Are they extremely cool? One day I would like to visit Canada, will you welcome me? It will be my pleasure to meet you my pen pal. Would you like to meet me too? I hope so. We will interact more.

From your lovely friend,
Adut Dau.

Have Nice Time.

Hey Brook pardy,

My name is Rita Bodi and am In grade ten at Morneau Sheppell girl's secondary school. I am exated to write to you these letter. I had "pen pals" but I have never had a "pen pal" out side Africa. Therefore I am happy to have you as my best friend ever in life.

Let me tell you about myself. I have been living In kakuma kenya since 2006. I am a Sudanese by nationality. I am living as aminor. My parents are In Sudan. I have seven siblings four sisters and three brothers. Our first born is In Australia U.S.A. The other sisters got married as the only girl in my family, I am the only girl who is educated; Imagined how life is clear?

My favourite subjects are History, Geography, Chemistry, Biology, kiswahili and English. I like the Sciences most because In future I want to be a Doctor. I admire the proffession and Iam always wishing and dreaming that my dreams will came true.

My hobbies is playing football and playing volleyball of course I have liked the games when I was young. It makes feelt that good when I exercise myself. I have a dog call Jimmy. I like it because when people are not around at home, he can remaind guiding tht house.

I hope we can be friends not only through letter but we can talked through Phones. My Telephone no is   . Iamso glad my dear for you being my friend.

From   Rita Bodi

118

February 11,ʳ,ᵗ 2015

Hi Rita Bodi,

I was thrilled to get your letter from
Clare last week and to be able to read about
your life in Kenya. I think it's fantastic
that you're pursuing an education and
want to be a doctor; I want to be a
doctor, too ☺ Maybe we could go to Medical
School together, one day!

How is the weather over there? Today it
was -11°C over here and it snowed beautiful,
fat snowflakes this afternoon when I was
coming home from school. I love winter
and playing in the snow, but I'm also
jealous of you guys over there, where the
weather is warmer and you never have to
worry about becoming ice and freezing
(not that it ever happens here ☺)!

How is Jimmy? I love that name for
a dog - it's nice, fun, and nappy, just like
a dog's name should be. How did you
decide on it? I've never had a dog before,
but when I was younger we had two
cats - one's name was Abby and the other's
name was Sam. Abby was the "bad"
cat, who would pee everywhere (sometimes
even in my room!), while Sam was the
nice cat, who liked to be petted and "meow".
I loved those cats and wish we could get
some new ones, but my brother is allergic of
any and all pets with fur, so we can't
have one. Two years ago, I was so
desperate for a pet that my friend and I
bought a red fish together from the
pet store. At first, we were really excited

about our fish, who we named Sebastian and sometimes called "Sebby". Overtime, though, we realized that fish are pretty boring and don't do much other than swimming, eating (he ate a lot!), and splashing. Still, we took good care of our fish, Sebastian, until last year when he passed away :(~~(there used to be a~~ ~~better fish, and we haven't had one since.)~~

    I bet you have some good stories about Jimmy :(- I love that name! I keep on saying it "Jimmy, Jimmy, Jimmy" - it's so cute :). I look forward to hopefully some of them and recieving your letter. It's amazing to be able to write this letter to you and to have you send me one back, even though we're so far away from each other, in different contenents! Good luck in the coming school year and say "hi" to Jimmy for me :

From,

    Brooke Pardy

PS. I hope you can read my writing - it's sort of messy!

  Sam   Abby   Jimmy   Sebastian (Sebby)

March 3, 2015

Dear Bashir,

It was amazing getting to talk to you on skype!
So to better get an understanding of my life,
I thought it would be a good idea to give
you a run-down of my daily life and the
activities I have each day. ☺

My Day in the Life of Vienna:

6 - 7am : Wake up (never fun so early)

8:20 : School Begins

- Period 1
- Period 2

11:50 - 12:50 : Lunch (hopefully a yummy descrt too)

- Period 3
- Period 4

3:30pm : School ends (walk home)

4 - 6pm : HOMEWORK (My favourite time of the day...)

6:30 - 8:30pm : Volleyball practice for my club team

9pm : Rest and get ready for bed!

Hopefully that gave you an idea about what my life is
usually like. I would love to learn about yours!
I can't wait to talk to you some time soon.

- Vienna ♡ xoxo

☺

Hi my name is Niki! I am 15 years old and am in grade 10. I live in Toronto, Canada with my two older sisters and my parents. My oldest sister's name is Simrin and she is currently studying to be a doctor. My other sister's name is Hannah and she is studying to become an engineer. Simrin is 21 years old and Hannah is 18 years old. I'm the youngest in my family. Do you have any siblings? My favourite subjects in school are Art and Science. I love to do art in my past time to take my mind off things. I also like to read books. What do you like to do in your free time? I enjoy playing sports to stay active, do you play any sports? The sports I play are rowing, soccer, cross country and field hockey.

Looking forward to hearing back from you!
Niki

My two sisters and I. Simrin is to the left and Hannah
Is to the right. I am in the middle of the picture.

This is my family. My parents are in the middle of the photo and I am on the right of the photo. My sister Simrin is on the left of the photo and Hannah is in the bottom middle.

This is my bestfriend. Her name is Alex and is standing to the left of me.

Hey Amina! ☺

I was so excited to recieve your letter!
Your family seems super cool! You said you
like to Sing and Dance. I love dancing, except
I'm horrible at singing. Do you have any
favorite songs, or musicians, or types of music?
Also, what kind of Dance do you like to do?
Wow, you also wrote that you play basketball!
That's so fun! You are very talented. Do you
like to do any arts? I take art at school and
right now were designing a stencil that we will
paint on to a t-shirt to wear. It's really cool + fun.
    Last week I just turned 16. ☺ That means
that I can now get my drivers license. I'm
excited to be able to drive! Whens your Birthday?
    I'm sorry to hear about your cat, that's
very sad ☹. I would be very sad if I lost my
kitty.
    I liked talking to you on the skype call.
I hope we do those more often.

    Looking Forward to hearing from you!

        From,
            Kate ☺

March 3, 2015

Hi Ruthrose!

How are you? ☺ I hope your New Year is good. Mine has been so hectic - school is so busy. How is school for you?

To answer your last letter, my favourite classes are Latin and Science! I sometimes like math, but I have a test today so I am not enjoying math as much.

Also, my birthday is coming up on March 10! I will be 16 and I am so excited!! when is your birthday?

March 4, 2015

I wish I could have seen you today at the Skype call this morning. I had to leave halfway through for a music lesson 🎵 But the lesson is for piano, which I absolutly love! I asked for you at the call, but maybe you weren't there or I wasn't clear. Either way, it was so cool to see the girls at your school - you are all so kind. What time was it when we called? Also, how do you fit 10 classes into 1 school day? We only have 4 classes everyday, and 8 classes in total. How long is your school day? Ours is 7 hours.

On a totally different topic, how are things? Anything new or exciting? It's nearly March break for us and I am excited. Also, my friend Emily says hi!

Much love,
Georgia

Dear Christine,

I am so fortunate to be partnered with an amazing, and outstanding young woman like you. Your story brought me an abundance of emotions, your truthful and captivating words brought me tears at times, and your words also made me smile because of your courage, perseverance, and ambition. No matter the distance between us I think we have many similarities in common, and I think our biggest similarity is we both want you to live the life you have always dreamt for and I will do anything I can to help with that, just let me know in the letters we write back and forth to each other. I have faith in you Christine that you will succeed, the only the factor of time is making each day move by so slow but with the exceptional goals and dreams that you have I promise you the days of waiting for your dream life to begin will only move faster. For now our words will connect us the best they can and so I am truly so appreciate for your honesty in what you write to me and I will respond to any questions you have.

We both have the zodiac sign of a cancer. The cancer is known to have character strengths of compassion, emotional sensitivity, determination, and the fierce protection of loved ones. You are blessed to have family close to you to love and protect. I hear you have two sisters, one age 25 and your step sister, as well as a nephew, two nieces, and a brother-in-law. How often do you get to see your family members? When reading your story, I saw religion was very important to you because you said it gives you the chance to fit into a society, I agree with you, religion allows for people to connect and creates a spiritual community with someone to go to for advice or help? You are so lucky to have a best friend like Harriet, she sounds wonderful and it is nice to have someone to talk to about anything, and be there in on check you. You mentioned that when living in the camp it is good knowing different languages, I am learning Spanish, but I want to learn more languages. I definitely agree that it is good to know other languages to communicate and meet new people and develop new friendships.

I want you to keep on dreaming, because when you know what you want you then know what you are working for. You are working hard in school so you can live in a place that you love and are happy in, a place will make you feel safe, and comfortable and allows you to help the others around you. You will live an inspiring life, and when you have kids they will be lucky to call you their mother, a mother that will be known as fearless, creative, loving, thoughtful, and powerful.

Like I said in the beginning of the letter, I want to be there for you and it would be a dream of mine like it is a dream if yours to go to a Canadian university and I have total faith in you that you can do it Christine, and I can be there beside you. You are so smart, genuine, kind, caring, and extremely brave and strong and I look forward to hearing more from you. If you have any questions about me, always ask and I will tell you anything about my life.

Sincerely,

Love. Stephanie Higgs <3

The World
According to Girls

Friendship
Sarah Nyajuok Gik
Georgia Gopinath

A friendship is an inseparable bond that people have. It is a bond that brings people together and makes them one, irrespective of their various differences such as their races. Friendship is also a relationship that two people have that occurs naturally.

The relationship I value so much is my relationship with my mom. My mom has taken good care of me ever since she gave birth to me up to now. Whenever I am sick she is with me. Whenever I need anything she makes sure that she provides for me, and whenever I am in trouble she is there beside me. She has never done anything that has made me feel that I am fatherless.

She has brought me up with a lot of love. She taught me good behaviour and has instilled in me good moral values. I am so lucky to have such a mother because if you consider the challenges she has gone through I am very sure that if it were for another woman she would have abandoned her child long ago. Nothing can break my friendship with my mother. She is my father, mother, and everything else.

I have really enjoyed my friendship with the Canadian girls so much. I have gotten to know how they live, how their education system works, and several other things. They have made me desire to go to Canada and meet them personally. They have encouraged me to continue working hard since I am hoping to get the opportunity to study at a higher level in Canada.

My friendship with Canadian girls has created in me more hope for my future. I can see the image of my success in life through you girls since you're the mirror of my success. Thanks!

CM: What does friendship mean to you?
GG: Friendship is just caring for each other and having each other's backs and having a good time with others.

CM: What's an example of a really strong friendship that you have?
GG: Well, I have a couple of friends that I've known since I was little and no matter what, even if we fight or don't talk for a couple of years, we've always ended up being friends and have grown closer than ever this year. It's really nice to build these kind of long-lasting friendships that endure anything.

CM: What have you learned from your different friendships?
GG: I have learned how to be compassionate towards more people because my friendships have helped me to think of others. For example, if one of my friends is going through a tough time but acts like all is fine, it makes me realize that people could be experiencing the same thing and that my kindness could help them. My friendships have also taught me how to be a good listener.

CM: Have you learned anything in particular from your friendship with the girls in Kakuma?
GG: It's really opened my eyes to make me more appreciative of what I have and has made me thankful for the bond of friendship. I feel like I have these friends in Kakuma and I care for them and think about them. It just makes me grateful for everything.

Weather

Adut Dau and Fardosa Ali Hassan
Sidney Wilson

Weather in Kakuma is harsh. High temperatures are experienced throughout the year as it is a semi-arid area. Low rainfall is also experienced sometimes, especially in April and August. During the day the temperatures are also high, which affects the afternoon duties. At school it becomes so hard to concentrate in class because of the high temperature, and at night the temperatures are so low it is cold when we try to sleep.

There is occasional flooding of the eroded gullies, which sometimes sweeps away houses and also carries people and animals. The flooding is very destructive.

During windy seasons especially in the month of February we experience hard times because it causes sand storms, which bury people and things. Some home chores like cooking are hard because the dust penetrates the windows. They are not closed because of the hot weather. Even at school it's hard to learn—the teachers strain when teaching and we have to struggle to pay attention.

[Fardosa's] country is Somalia, which has a different weather from Kakuma because most of the months in the year the weather is calm and cloudy, and the temperatures are moderate.

CM: So tell us a little bit about the weather in Canada.

SW: Canada is very cold, like everybody says, but it's not cold all the time. There are warm periods of time, like in the summer when it gets quite warm, up to thirty degrees. It's not much different from a lot of areas in the United States. At least where I live, it gets really cold. It's quite a dry area where I live, but there are other areas, like coastal Canada, British Columbia, or in the Maritimes that are a lot wetter and a lot more temperate, especially in British Columbia. We can get quite a bit of snow in the winter.

CM: Depending where you are in winter, like in Nunavut in the Arctic, it can get as cold as -40°C. Toronto's not that extreme but when there is a lot of snow, do you ever find that the weather can make getting an education difficult for you?

SW: I wouldn't say exactly that it makes getting an education difficult for me, but I live in a family with a lot of kids, and so I walk to and from school every day, so especially in the winter and in the rain, it's hard to get to and from school. There's public transportation that people can take to get to school but even then, in the winter it gets a lot slower, because of the snow. A lot of the time people are late for school or there are even snow days sometimes, where the school shuts down because there is too much snow. It's just a lot more effort to get to school. I don't know what it's like in Africa where it is really windy and hot, or how far you have to walk to school.

Home

Zahira Habila Ariss
Zoë Mcdonald and Alie Hunter

A home means a great place in my life where I stay, and which I depend on for survival. It means where I live in peace and harmony with my beloved ones.

A home also is a place I always remember, whatever circumstances and conditions I am experiencing. I find it as the only place where I come to understand fully about life and the principles needed for my prosperity. That is why I have fully developed passion for it.

A home can also mean a place of origin; where I originated, grew up, and acquired all the necessities of life. It means a place where I find comfort and support and where all my rights are in place. Home is where no one at all interferes with my being and I am granted an opportunity to experience all my likes and dislikes in life.

My home is anywhere I can meet all my basic and secondary needs. It does not matter to me at all where it is located. But what matters a lot to me is my peace and harmony with other people and myself.

My home is where my parents and relatives are living currently. And that is in Sudan where I came into being and thrived. Currently, I live in Kakuma Refugee Camp and that is where my home is, but that does not mean it is my permanent home.

My home can also be anywhere my mind rests and I am comfortable to live. And it will be much better to me if I am where I can share ideas and experiences with other people. That will actually be my lovable home.

CM: Where is home to you?

AH: For me, I think home is not a physical place but a place where there are people that I love and care about and who care about me, and I can be myself.

ZM: I also think it has a lot to do with places that you are familiar and comfortable with, and like Alie said, where you have memories of people you love.

CM: Why do you think your home is important to you? Why do you need a home?

AH: I think you need someplace or someone you can go back to and you can be yourself without anyone else.

CM: So it's like a secure place?

AH: Yeah.

ZM: I agree. It's just somewhere you can go back to and feel safe and at home.

Clare: And who do you need—do you need friends, family—who do you need in your life to make it your home?

AH: I think you need friends, and I think you need family, but I think you need people who care for you and know and look out for your best interests.

ZM: I think you need your family to actually be in your home with you, but friends can come over and be supportive and share memories with you.

CM: So then how would you feel if you didn't have a home? If you didn't have that sense of security?

ZM: I think it would be hard to feel comfortable.

AH: I think you lose your sense of belonging and identity. You wouldn't really know who you were or what you were a part of. I think it would be hard to find yourself if you didn't know where you came from.

CM: And do you think the school you go to or your religious beliefs or your afterschool activities influence your home and how you feel about your community?

AH: Yes. I think they make you stronger.

ZM: I guess that having outside experience strengthens your home aspect.

AH: It allows you to have a bunch of different homes and a bunch of different places where you feel comfortable, and a bunch of new 'families'.

School Life
Ruthrose Emmanah and Esther Nyakong
Alexia Lucas

Apart from academics there are so many activities we do enjoy in school. Every Monday evening and Wednesday we have sports. On Tuesday we have clubs such as science and mathematics club, journalism, scouts, movement, and society.

Our morning sessions start at 4:30 am, when students wake up. We prepare for thirty minutes and go for a morning study session, and then we work on our assignments for one hour.

At 6:00 am we have our breakfast for twenty minutes and we break for manual work for thirty minutes. I always like this moment because students finish their work on time and go for morning lessons.

Our lessons always run for forty minutes in each subject. We enjoy science lessons and mathematics because it is all about our life. We have a short break between 8:45 am and 9:05 am, a tea break from 10:50 am to 11:10 am, and a lunch break from 1:00 pm to 1:30 pm. After lunch we always have afternoon lessons to 3:30 pm where we break for clubs and then for self-care.

Every Saturday afternoon we have entertainment (e.g., listening to music and watching Nigerian movies). We also have debate every Thursday. In our school we have music club and singing clubs also. We really enjoy interacting with each other, and sharing our ideas and culture.

CM: What do you enjoy about school life other than academics—so sports, activities, anything other than your classes?

AL: I would definitely say sports. I have played sports at Havergal every year that I've been here. I've played every level of field hockey at Havergal and I love that. I really like the arts at Havergal too. I think Havergal does a really good job of running arts programs, although I am less involved with these programs. I often go watch Havergal's artistic groups and productions, even when I am not a part of them.

CM: What is the arts program like at Havergal?

AL: I take visual arts now and I've taken it since grade nine. Visual arts focuses mainly on drawing and painting, but it sometimes incorporates working with clay and even carving rocks.

CM: Are you in any clubs at Havergal?

AL: I'm in pre-med club because I want to be a doctor. It's fun so far, even though we have only had one meeting. I'm also in the film society, which is a lot of fun.

CM: Are there any other parts of school that you like?

AL: I'm actually in several community partnerships, which I really enjoy. Last year I was in the Red Cross partnership, which was really interesting because we focused on the Ebola crisis. We made a lot of posters and made sure that people were informed about the crisis. I was also in the Kakuma Toronto Girls Education Partnership last year and had this really sweet partner named Rose. I always reread the letters that she wrote to me. I was also in the Cancer Education Group, which was also interesting because we had people come in from outside the school.

War and Peace

Esther Nyakong
Kate Whibbs

Hello! Carol! Clare! How are you doing over there and the rest of the Havergal girls? Please send my greetings to them and I miss you so much.

Well, we all know that peace is the most important thing in life and it's like most Africans do not have knowledge of it. Where there is peace, there is love, understanding, respect, and good relations between people.

To turn to war, it is the cause of me and my fellow friends being refugees. Actually war is caused when a country lacks understanding and peace. I personally have experienced a lot. I have watched many people dying in war. I have slept next to them and passed through so much.

During war many people lose their lives, homes, and even their families. A lot of families have been torn apart by war. My questions are: How do you maintain peace in your country? How do you prevent war? What is it that you guys have and we lack? Why is it that we Africans are always fighting?

I have always thought of being a Canadian. I love your culture, traditions, and values. It is not that I do not like ours—in fact I love them. I have thought of leaving Africa one day and becoming the most famous lady in the world. Will Africa, especially my country (South Sudan), ever stop fighting and live in peace and harmony? I hope God will answer my prayers one day and make a change in South Sudan. Not only in my country, actually but in all of Africa.

Anyway I may have a lot to say but can't write all my thoughts. That's all for now. Have a nice time there! Love you! Oh! And please don't forget to greet my friend Chantal from Havergal, Toronto.

Living in Canada, peace is a word I am very familiar with. From living in peace in my community, to Canada being advertised as a peacekeeping nation, the idea of peace has become a topic very close to home. With this said, peace is not something I put much thought into. It is a word and idea I have grown up my whole life with, and therefore I don't really think about, or cannot imagine what my life would be like otherwise. When I do think or wish for peace, I am wishing for peace somewhere far from where I call home. Sadly, when I think how peace is present in my life, I see how taken for granted it has become. All I know and imagine for my future is living in a peaceful community.

On the other hand, war is something I know nearly nothing about. Everything I know about war today I have learned from watching the news or from history class. My closest ties to any type of war are from at least two generations back. My grandmother has been telling me her stories from growing up and escaping Germany during World War II since I was very small, and since then I have imagined them in a fairy tale sense. In my imagination, she was not the small girl escaping the Russian soldiers, but it was rather a make-believe character. I believe this was because she told me of her stories, but I could not actually connect her to them. She had lived in Canada, in peace, for the last fifty years, and I could not imagine anything else for her.

War is still a very scary and real thing to me. I don't believe I am completely safe from the effects of war. Effects from war can be felt from thousands of miles away. However, to actually fear war in my country would be considered an irrational fear by most. It is very hard for me to imagine living through it. It is incredible that I cannot even begin to understand what it is like to do so, yet there are so many girls my age who are experiencing it.

Refugees
Amach Mabior and Christine Bachoke

Refugees are people like anybody in the world. They are people who flee their countries because of different reasons such as war, famine, and internal and external conflict, searching for resolutions in other countries or continents.

Life for a refugee girl is not good because she faces a lot of problems due to her state of being a refugee. Everyone takes advantage of refugee girls. A refugee girl passes through many challenges, which are highlighted below.

First and foremost, many refugee girls are living alone in the camps due to circumstances such as being orphaned or having left behind their parents while fleeing their country. It creates problems, especially when girls who had been staying with their parents start living alone. This really challenges girls a lot. You will not be able to know where to start and where to end exactly because you are not used to it.

Secondly, the terrible thing that disorders girls is when your parents die and you become the head of the family, the one taking care of the other kids. This really challenges girls because we are young and need to give parental support to our siblings. This is what usually discourages girls from education. They stop aiming for a better future, hence giving up on their lives.

Lastly, girls get discouraged about their education by getting married in order to continue supporting and assisting their siblings so they can have a future. A young girl will be stressed out due to parental responsibilities at an early age. The stress they have makes them grow old faster. You cannot differentiate the old woman from the young, recently married girl because of the stresses they are passing through.

All in all, refugee girls are mistreated because of the status they possess. They can experience terrible things, like being raped and being beaten up ruthlessly simply because they are called refugees. It is very bad to be called refugee because people misinterpret it and it sounds terrible. The word refugee is very painful to us. We feel hopeless when we are called refugees because that is where the mistreatment comes from.

In conclusion, the world should not think that refugees are something strange. We are people like you, only we live in exile and lack freedom and we need more support for us to make a bright future. We all wish that one day we will not be refugees but citizens in our own homeland.

200?	1238	754	1992	May
2008	692	1322	3014	June 87
2009	3056	2569	5625	July
2010	5206	4294	9500	Augus.
2011	4514	3368	7882	Sept
2012	8922	6380	15302	October
2013	10836	7299	18135	Nov.
2014	24,182	23,832	48,014	Dec.
2015	2,425	1,682	4,107	TOTAL
TOTAL				

Kakuma Refugee Camp Reception Centre, chart of New Annual Arrivals up to July 2015

Education
Lula Abdulkhadir and Rita Monday Tom
Megan Stellato

Education is the key to success. It is an invaluable and priceless thing that cannot be compared to anything else. You can go anywhere with it. For us we believe that education can change our lives for the best. Somebody might want to rob you but they cannot rob the knowledge you have gotten from education.

Education is something that makes you become a better person in the world. It can change your behaviour from bad to good. You can acquire things that somebody who is not educated cannot acquire.

Girls are facing many challenges to acquire education, especially the day scholars. Girls are really depended on by their families to do house chores. Early in the morning before school they have to ensure that they have washed the utensils, cleaned the house, and prepared breakfast for the family. This makes most of the girls unable to attend the early morning classes due to late arrival. Some then leave the house without taking anything to eat, and then rush to school with an empty stomach.

Reaching school, they don't even know where to start and where to continue because their fellow classmates are already ahead of them. At lunchtime, they are forced to go home and take lunch. Some even have to walk five kilometres to go home and come back.

In the evening, house chores are still waiting for them. They have to cook dinner, fetch water, clean the house, and take care of their siblings. This gives them no time for revision.

The other challenge is that some girls miss

school because they have to go collect rations. On certain dates people are supposed to go for rations because on certain dates the food is being distributed to all the refugees in the camp. Those students who are minors without their parent representative are all alone and are supposed to go for the distribution.

Some girls are being raped while they are on their way to school. Some even get killed. This discourages many girls from going to school.

Early marriage is one of the most common challenges to girls. Girls are being forced to leave school by their parents and get married. Parents sometimes lack money to sustain them and they often try to get their daughters married and get money in the form of dowry. Some parents even threaten their daughters that they are going to curse them.

Early pregnancy is also one of the things that is making girls drop out of school. Some are cheated on by their boyfriends, who tell them they will provide them with everything. Because of poverty girls allow boys to do anything with them and hence girls get pregnant and drop out of school.

Girls' education is very important because it helps to eliminate poverty. As they say, educating a girl is like educating a whole nation.

Girls' education motivates us to dream big and can help us meet people. It gives us hope and courage on how to build a family in some years to come. It also helps me to educate those who are uneducated and help the poor who are unable to raise their life as well.

Education can take you anywhere. Like for us it was only through education that has made us meet the Havergal girls. Girls staying in the community do not have this opportunity.

Education can change a girl's life, together with her family's and her community peers'. It can bring light to a place that is full of darkness. Thank you a lot.

Why is education important to me? What does it mean to me?

When you set the bar high and you have goals you want to achieve, education plays a huge role in helping you to achieve those goals. Education is not only about sitting in a classroom and learning math. Schools help push you mentally and even physically. They encourage you and assist you in accomplishing your dreams.

Education has opened up many doors for me and provides me with knowledge of the world around me. It helps me to form and understand my own opinions and provides me with different points of view on many aspects in life. Education is the process of gaining knowledge and information about our surroundings, and it makes me capable of interpreting the things I perceive correctly. I want to be able to expand my intellectual comfort zone and stretch myself to the best of my abilities. Getting a good education is also about attending an institution where you feel comfortable, one that encourages you to see that your coursework is grounded in the real world. My dream is to make a difference in the world. By taking on the challenges and being inspired by the things education will bring to me, I believe I can do it.

In grade eight, I decided to show my parents how much a good education means to me. I did some research and I just knew that Havergal was the right school for me. I downloaded the application online and filled it out without my parents knowing. I then went on to study for the SSAT test, which I had signed myself up for. My parents eventually found out that I did this behind their backs. They were not angry; they simply believed I wouldn't get in. Those three months waiting to hear from Havergal for either my acceptance or decline letter were tough, but I worked harder than ever. I got accepted, and to this day, I do not take education for granted.

Spirituality
Nhial Alek Tabitha and Fardosa Ali Hassan
Emma Buckles

Religion is important because it enables you to think critically and make appropriate social, moral, and spiritual decisions. It also helps to form a bridge for further studies and career development.

I practice my religion by going to church and worshipping the Lord through singing in choir and watering the trees of the church. In school I sing worship songs and praises to honour him. I also act as a person who is experienced in the work of the Lord. In school mostly I take God as my personal saviour who can guide me in whatever I do in life. Through Christianity I [Nhial] have learned that love is the most important thing to be acquired from religion.

I have learned the importance of sharing our properties with others to live in harmony to sustain life. Unity in religion is also important, as it makes people into one family. I have learned the responsibilities I should carry out in life, and to be faithful.

I have learned to be tolerant and patient so I can achieve my goals in the future.

CM: Are you spiritual?
EB: Yes, I have been Catholic since I was a baby.

CM: How does your religion influence your life? What activities do you do surrounding your religion?
EB: We do the typical things. We go to mass every Sunday. For community service hours, and just to help out my cottage community, I actually served at the altar of my local church in Muskoka. I have also gone through the whole confirmation process. It's really something I have been brought up into.

CM: So what does your religion mean to you?
EB: That's a difficult question, Clare! That's really a wide scheme of things to think about. It's really just the belief in an upper being. It's a huge thing to believe that someone is watching you and having all these ideals that everyone believes in. To hope that there is something is a big thing.

CM: So do you think your religion influences or gives you a path or support in any way?
EB: Yeah, it's definitely something. You're hoping that you have this ideal path and for a reason someone is watching you or your past family members are watching you. It's definitely something that supports you in hard times and even good times. You always have reasoning behind why something happens.

CM: How has your religion helped you become closer to your family, community, or Havergal?
EB: From the beginning, as kids, it was definitely a shared thing between my family and a smaller community. I know my cottage community is close-knit—we have church activities that everyone goes to. It turns into a social event, but of course it's all based around this idea that has been originated back in history. So, it does have its social connections, which is a nice thing, especially when you get older. I think it will be a thing that will keep us connected.

Family

Amach Mabior and Zahira Habila Ariss
Tory Robertson

Our families are well-organized and composed of both males and females. Our families are headed by males, either by a father or an eldest son, as it is believed that males are superior to females, which is not the case. The woman's dignity is sometimes undermined in our families because of traditional customs.

Most of our families are polygamous as it is believed that children are a source of wealth and security. That is why many parents produce as many children as they can. This is why most of our families experience poverty, as the duty of caring for us becomes a burden to them. The poverty we experience leads us to drop out of school because our needs cannot be met. People live according to their families' rules and laws, which guide them to do what is right and acceptable in the family.

Our families have several important roles in our lives. Some are highlighted below.

Firstly, they ensure continuity of life. When a person dies, if they have left behind children, those children ensure that the lineage of the family continues. People feel nice when their names are used to name young children. They know that their names will not fade, so they will be remembered forever in the family and their lineage will never come to an end.

In addition, family property is mostly inherited by the eldest son and the rest of sons also get a portion of the family property. The eldest son also inherits the position of the father in terms of leadership when the father dies. This is passed on from generation to generation. The girls on the other side do not inherit anything because they will obviously move away from their families and join other families, so they are supposed to inherit things wherever they are going.

Families provide support to one another in terms of basic needs, medicine, and security. The family also provides support in terms of guidance and counselling in order to grow morally upright and be of good minds and thoughts. Our families are always supportive in spite of not having many resources—they try as they can to make us feel wanted in the family. The family is always protective in order to make sure that the family members are all safe.

Lastly, a polygamous family is more advantaged compared to a monogamous family in terms of security in times of difficulty, and they also make their family names famous. The sons protect the family members and girls provide labour to the family and also bring wealth in terms of bride price.

CM: Describe your family.

TR: I have three siblings, all of whom are younger than me. Scott is twelve, Coco is ten, and William is six. William is like my baby—he's a little Mini Me. He's very small and very cute. I love all of my siblings so much, and I really love my parents. I also love my dog, Gary, who's twelve. Scott plays competitive hockey. He's really good at it and loves it a lot. Coco loves skiing and William plays soccer. All of my siblings are smart and do very well in school. My younger sister Coco goes to the same school as me and Scott and William go to different schools. My dog is also a really important part of my family. I love walking him.

CM: What is the importance of family to you?

TR: I think family is so important. Your family is your support system and you need your family to support and challenge you. They build your beliefs and your confidence. I think your family is really important in creating your character and that you are a reflection of your family's values. It's important to have a strong connection with your family because at the end of the day, your family members are the only ones that are there for you 100 per cent.

CM: How has your family shaped who you are?

TR: We do a lot of things together. We have family movie nights together usually every Sunday night, or every so often, and we watch different cooking shows or random things together. All the kids in my family are different ages, and we're different, but we still like watching the same shows together.

I think the support my family has given me has given me confidence. Without them, I don't think that I would be as confident as I am. Without them backing me up, I think my self-esteem would be a lot lower.

Like all parents' values do, my parents' values have shaped me.

Culture

Nyimuch Chuol Wel
Stephanie Higgs

In my culture, we don't practice circumcision of males or females. Males have six lines cut on their forehead using a knife as a sign of childhood to adulthood, and females are tattooed using a needle and a razor blade, as a sign of beauty.

The initiation could put someone's life in danger because cutting the forehead leads to severe bleeding and causes anemia.

In terms of marriage, a man has to pay a hundred heads of cattle and must have the six marks on his forehead in order to marry the girl. The marriage is carried out such that a young calf is slaughtered first for the elders.

The women cover only their front private parts with a hide of a goat while men go more nude, with white paint on their bodies.

My culture is important because it reminds me of how life was a long time ago.

I stay connected to my culture by attending some of the cultural activities that still exist, like dances. I have visited Tobong'lore Cultural Centre where the Turkana show their mode of dressing, food, and culture.

In Morneau Shepell Secondary School for Girls I've learned that more cultures, like the Somalis, practice female genital mutilation and the Sudanese don't. Turkana women dress in hides of animals and the Acholi of Sudan dress in beads.

CM: Can you tell us about culture in Canada?
SH: In Canada, I find that we are community-centred. We are dedicated to helping one another. I know that people may contradict this, but I believe that by paying taxes, we're helping one another because that allows us to have things such as free healthcare. I also think that although we have a lot of stereotypical views of Canadians, like igloos and plaid and maple syrup, I find that as a culture we're very diverse. I think I have been lucky to grow up in Toronto, where I have been surrounded by so many cultures. There are even areas of Toronto dedicated to certain cultures, like Little Italy and Chinatown. I think that I'm interested in Kakuma because it has allowed me to broaden my perspective even more.

CM: What new cultures have you learned about at Havergal?
SH: It is hard because Havergal has historically been a school with a very white background, so sometimes it is hard to experience different cultures at Havergal. However, in grade eight, we did a project where we had to connect to our roots and our backgrounds and do a presentation on it. I found it really interesting because some girls who were from India or whose parents were from China did presentations on those countries, which helped me learn more about their cultures.

CM: And how do you stay connected to Canadian culture?
SH: I stay connected to Canadian culture by participating in all the holidays that we have throughout the year in Canada. Canada Day is a very important day and I don't think that's just because of the fireworks. It is about being with friends and remembering how lucky we are to live in the country we live in. It can get complicated at times but I know there are always supportive people surrounding me and I always appreciate the way I am able to live. Another way that I think I connect with Canada is by giving back. For example, I know that global warming is a big issue in the world right now. In Canada we're so lucky to have the agricultural land that we do, so by buying from local farmers and markets, we help support our fellow Canadians and avoid pollution.

CM: What cultural landscapes and places in Canada are important to you?
SH: Growing up, my dad and I would go on trips to Algonquin Park every year, in June or July. That is really where I felt the most in my place, because we would canoe, hike, be outdoors, and cook fresh food over a fire. It was stunning to see this land, which is so unlike Toronto. I find Toronto can be similar to many other cities, like Chicago, because it has the tall buildings, the streets, and the tourist industry, but there is no place like Algonquin Park and the wilderness parks we have throughout Canada.

I went to camp for seven years and I think a favourite part of that was doing canoe portages and being with friends. You learn a lot of leadership skills and you learn how to be independent. Being taken away from technology is really peaceful.

The Future

Christine Bachoke and Sarah Nyajuok Gik

Emma Bray

We would like to thank you once more for granting us a chance to express ourselves and tell you more about our future.

To begin with, the fears of our future. Actually things that we fear are: Losing of dreams. Sometimes we sit and ask ourselves whether we shall reach our goals and objectives, but for that question, we tell ourselves we can through God's help and through the people who care most for us, like our friends in Canada and so on. Also we do fear that the world is too big for us when we are being looked down on because of our status. But we remember that if even Jesus was a refugee, who are we to be discouraged? It helps us to go on.

Surely, we have many hopes for our future. We hope that in our future never shall we be called the names that we are called now, but in future we shall have names of honour. All this is possible through our education, especially after we have joined Morneau Shepell School for Girls. It built our hope and we believe our hopes will be fulfilled.

Moreover, we have dreams for us, our countries, and the globe. Christine dreams of being an engineer or a professional writer. Sarah dreams of being a model or a pilot in her future. We dream that we shall finish high school with better grades and join the next level. We dream of the world changing for the better: We hope one day it will support the needy, and our countries will stop warring and fight against famine, illiteracy, and poverty.

Lastly, we would like to see ourselves in comfortable places with comfortable lives that can at least make us forget what we have passed through. We will never wish to see our children living the kind of life we lived. We also wish to see the world become better, so everyone feels they are in a better place.

We hope you will continue being with us and you will continue supporting us to reach our goals, fulfill our dreams, and be what we need to be in the future.

Despite my best efforts to enjoy the possibility the future brings, thinking of my unknown future induces a panic in me. I end up trying to focus on one goal for the future, something I can direct all of my work toward. There is a single thing that continues to encourage me that I know I need to aim for: Passion.

During my short sixteen years I have been able to come to a few valuable conclusions. One that has actually affected my life is the importance of passion. Whether it is for a cause, a person, or work, passion transforms your life. Being able to fully throw yourself into your chosen topic is exhilarating, and is the one trait I believe a satisfying future must include. Now when I plan for my future, I have a more tangible goal. I hope to have a career, whatever

it might be, that is important to me and I feel has a true purpose. I hope to have a family of my own that I can work hard for, and one that loves me. I also hope that everyone has the same opportunity that I have to work for a passionate life.

Another reason passion is such an important part of life is that it is accessible from any political, social, or economic standpoint an individual may find themselves in. The love of what you do is not dependent on your status. Passion is not something that can be handed to you— you have to discover it for yourself. When I look ahead to the future, I hope for a world where everyone realizes the importance of passion and is able to take full advantage of every opportunity thrown at them.

Wisdom for the Future

Interview with Panther Kuol
Clare Morneau

Panther Kuol has a story that is representative of so many Lost Boys—he walked for miles from South Sudan to Kakuma Refugee Camp without his parents. Panther is truly one of my heroes. He has experienced a lot of violence and death in his life, yet he has managed to grow into a gentle, caring human being. He is a living inspiration for many of the refugee students in Kakuma, and for me and many of my peers.

Panther has been incredibly supportive during the creation of the Kakuma Toronto Girls Education Partnership and the process of writing this book. When I first told Panther that I was writing a book about Kakuma Refugee Camp, he immediately told me that he would love to help in any way possible. I thought that the best way for him to help was for him to tell his story—his story and his words attest to his wonderful personality more than I ever can. During the interview, he would stop every now and then to make sure that I understood everything, and he insists to this day that I email him whenever I have any questions about Kakuma Refugee Camp. Panther's experience can't

represent a refugee girl's experience but he speaks as a Canadian who grew up in Kakuma Refugee Camp.

CM: What is your story? How did you end up in Kakuma? How did you leave the camp?
PK: Back in South Sudan, there was a civil war that began in '83. I was a little one the year it started. Our villages kept getting under attack from the government militia. One day we couldn't take it, we couldn't keep hiding because the government was attacking from the air and attacking from the ground, so we just ran. We left in a group with some of the boys from the village and we just walked. The few elders that were with us guided us and they kept telling us that we were going up. "Up" turned out to be a neighbouring country. We ended up in Ethiopia after about a month of walking on foot, and you know with all the dangers, there are no roads, so you literally go into the bushes. So, at six years old, I found myself in my first refugee camp. I became a refugee.

I lived there for three years and then that country became destabilized again. There was war in the country that I went to hide in, because you know that region of Africa is infected with conflict. I left again and went back to my country. I stayed there as an internally displaced person, so I didn't go back to my village, just stayed at the border. Then I went to Kakuma Refugee Camp in 1992. I was ten years old. Again, we had walked from another country back to South Sudan, and from South Sudan to Kenya, all on foot. It was a struggle because there was no support on the way, because we lost some of our friends because they couldn't carry on or were sick. There were no doctors. Some became thirsty or died of hunger, but I was incredibly lucky to survive and to arrive in the camp. So that's how I ended up in Kenya, which was my second country of refuge.

I enrolled in a UN school that was first conducted under trees. My first class in Kakuma was under trees. The teacher at first did not have a board, and he would only give instructions. We would write in the dirt and the teacher would go around marking. So it was a very humble beginning, and we continued from there.

If you went back to Kakuma today, it's much different. There are modern buildings. Some of the classes have changed from under the trees to grass-thatched buildings. It is still modest. The walls are made with mud so when it rains, they can easily collapse, and there have been classes that collapsed in the camp because of their poor structure.

We kept up hope. Obviously there was no other life to compare it to. Looking back, I would obviously think that I had been through a tough time, but back then it was all fun. The opportunity to go to school was fun; playing with kids was fun. It wasn't a bother, we were safe. That was one big thing. Being in the camp, you would not feel insecure. Even though there have been instances of crime in Kakuma, it was

relatively safe because you're out of the war zone. That was my journey from my village in South Sudan, which was Bor, to Ethiopia, and from Ethiopia back to South Sudan because Ethiopia was destabilized, and from there to Kenya, where I was lucky to be received by UNHCR. All my life, during that time, and when I lived in the camp for thirteen years, I was supported by UNHCR. Everything, every living thing that you use to support yourself, like food, water, shelter, was distributed by the UN, until I got the opportunity to come here.

CM: So what was the education like in the camp? Was it hard to get an education?
PK: It was hard. Like I said, the facilities were really in poor shape. There were not enough books, so you would use one exercise book for like three courses, and once it's filled up, you don't have a replacement. They give you one pen, and if it runs out of ink, that's it. The same with pencils—there were never enough. The scarcity of resources was evident. In terms of attending the school and motivating myself to excel in classes, it was not difficult. It was fun because I got good grades and I kept working through the support of my teachers and their encouragement. Through hardships, I worked very hard. We would study in the night There's no electricity in the camp, so we would use candles and sometimes kerosene lamps. It can be really painful when you have one lamp and ten kids all sitting around to prepare for exams. Educational equipment and resources are scarce, but a few books made it all worthwhile, and I got the best of it.

CM: And how did you get to Canada?
PK: I came through a program called World University Service of Canada, WUSC. WUSC goes around many different places in the world

where there are refugees and they interview through local organizations. They identify refugees who have the credentials to attend university but are lacking funds to support their schooling. I was one candidate interviewed by WUSC out of more than five hundred. WUSC would take around twenty-five from the camp. These were people from different nations, so it was a very fierce competition, if you consider all of the criteria. They have to consider the number of girls, they have to consider different nationalities of refugees that are presented to make sure that it is diverse and catering to all sectors of the communities in the camp. So I came through World University Service of Canada. It's actually incredible because this program is supported by students in Canada. In 1982 at Simon Fraser, which I later attended, students passed a referendum saying that when they pay school fees, each one of them, each student, would pay an extra levy of 75 cents. Considering there are over 30,000 students, that adds up and helped support my schooling for the first year. The program is also in collaboration with Immigration Canada, so I became a permanent resident when I landed in Canada. That gave me opportunities to support myself like any other student. The opportunity to become a permanent resident and to leave the camp through this program required huge luck on my part. It could have been any other refugee.

CM: So education in the camp, and getting to a university is a dream? In Canada, a lot of kids take it for granted, but in the camp, you would think it would be the goal, like what kids hold on to?
PK: Yes, exactly. It's a big goal and I can tell you that a lot of kids become motivated to work harder because they know that if they have the

grades, there is this program that has the opportunity to bring them to Canada. It's a dream, it's like winning a lottery. I don't consider myself more worthy than any other refugee who has the grades. I consider it luck, I consider it a privilege, and in any way possible, I can never be content. I should want to give back because someone else has sacrificed to make this happen for me.

CM: What would you think would be most needed in the camp to help more refugee children go to university?
PK: The kids living in the camp deserve better classrooms to help them get to university. They need to withstand the appalling conditions in the camp. It's a very dusty town. If you talk about environmental challenges, in terms of water, in terms of the green environment, this is the face of it. This is the hottest part of Kenya. Anything that will help change the classrooms inside the camp and also the living conditions, like the type of houses that refugees live in, the water sources, these kinds of things, to make life acceptable in the camp would be valuable. As you see, as I go around in Canada, there's an ad that I see about breakfast in schools. This is something that is important. If a kid is hungry, they will not be able to study well. Sometimes, since there are so many refugees, the UN can only do so much. UNHCR relies on the generosity of others, and because there are so many conflicts in the war, UNHCR resources are scarce. So, if kids can be fed well, if they can sleep well, if they can have better classrooms, this can help them perform well, because the World University Program of Canada takes into account academic merit. So for them to do well, you need to make sure they have a better quality of life at home.

CM: Yes, it takes a really resilient student to push through that. Do you think the difficulty with weather affects school life?

PK: Well, sometimes, if you're in a class and the wind just blows all day in your face, blows with dirt, this can be really physically uncomfortable, particularly to withstand that coming into your face when you're attending class. So, just to have better structures. And it's extremely hot, so if they could have fans or air conditioning, even better. I know that electricity infrastructure is really poor in the camp, so there is only so much that can be done. You would have to change the entire infrastructure around the town of Kakuma.

The key is to have classroom resources available and to have teachers trained better. I think that would help them in the immediate sense. In terms of environment, it's a very bad environment, in terms of how climate change and the conditions are. I cannot say how that would be

easily addressed. You cannot change the weather or the environment or the conditions, but you can prepare people to withstand those by making conditions more favorable in terms of fans, better infrastructure, and improved house construction. Also, they need to plant more trees in the camp, so that is something that students can be inspired to do. They can be encouraged to plant more trees. I believe that between 1992 and the time I left Kakuma, it became greener than when we found it. That is through encouraging people to live a green life.

CM: So obviously there are weather challenges and challenges with school infrastructure, but what about after school? Do kids play sports? Do they have any activities?

PK: Yes, they have activities, but it's not as organized or as planned out as I see here,

because here in Canada you have after-school programs. Those are clear programs where kids go to swimming classes or do ballet or sit on different sports teams. For me personally, my experience was that I played soccer after classes. There are no soccer balls. They might have them in shops but they were very expensive and we couldn't afford them. So what we did, because it's very important to play and be able to forget everything you're going through because it can make people hopeful in desperate situations, so we made our soccer balls out of balloons. We blow it up and wrap pieces of clothing on it. We actually used bandages to protect it because there are thorns in the camp and the 'ball' could easily rupture. We'd put a lot of clothing on it and put it in socks and twist it and make it round and that's what we used for a ball. Sometimes, when we didn't have the balloons, we would put pieces of clothes and make them into a ball. So playing was a big part

of entertaining kids. There wasn't much else. There are no parks to play in. I just remember kids doing simple things. If it rained a bit, people would do something similar to tobogganing, but it's not real, because you're playing in the mud. Sports are an important thing in Kakuma—they really help inspire. By the time I left the camp, there were basketball courts, volleyball courts, a lot of soccer fields around. It's gender-encompassing as well, so girls are able to play as well. In some cultures, girls only have access to certain things based on their gender and that's problematic, so it's good to see that all students are able to take advantage of sports. Obviously the girls are still doing work at home, so when they are at home they are more disadvantaged than their brothers, because they have to do all the work, but the sports activities are there. The equipment is still lacking, so if schools can provide those, I'm sure kids would take most advantage of it.

CM: On the topic of food, how does that work in the camp? How do you get and make food?

PK: Every fifteen days, UNHCR gives out food rations. Every refugee is registered—it's like having a SIN card here—so you are identified by your ID and you show up. It's not a food bank, but you show up at this place where they give you your food ration for fifteen days. They give out maize or corn and beans, oil, salt. They give you all those little things and it's up to you to ration it for fifteen days. If you run out, there are no food courts, there's no way you can borrow, there's nothing else. I saw that some elders would go on one meal per day, to make sure that the food they have is enough for the kids for fifteen days. How you make that work varies from family to family. There are some families where one is able to earn a modest income. For example, I was a volunteer teacher in high school and they would give me $40 a month. That helped a bit. I would give that to Mum and she could buy a few things, buy meat, because they don't distribute that. They only give you the imperishable foods, so they don't give you vegetables, so you don't get a balanced diet from the UN. You can only supplement by selling part of the rations that you've been given so you can get vegetables and stuff. I don't think it has changed.

CM: Yeah, I've talked to some girls living in the camp now and it's still the same. Some of them will say that their food will run out so they will have to wait and go for three days without food because they want their brothers to eat instead.

PK: Their little brothers.

CM: Yes, their little brothers. Especially some girls because they're not with their parents in the camp. And on that, do you still have family and friends in the camp now?

PK: Yes, I do. I have relatives. My mother is actually still registered as a refugee but I can afford to pay for her rent in Nairobi. That's the only reason she is not there, but I still have lots of other relatives who are living through the same conditions in the camp.

CM: And would you hope to one day bring some of your friends, or have some of your friends come to Canada?

PK: Well, my number-one issue, since I know that Canada offers great opportunities for people and it's impossible for me to bring my entire family, my main hope is to have peace in my country. We have a beautiful country that if we could end war, if people could stop fighting, these refugees would go back and do farming for themselves, to be able to do businesses and prosper. So that is my number one hope, but if conditions don't change, because it seems like every year things keep getting worse and worse back there, well I have a home here and I feel very privileged to be here in Canada. I would love to have members of my family or my friends enjoy the same privileges that I have here, but it's not possible for me to bring all of them. Definitely they would appreciate the good health care we have in this country, and to be able to live in a peaceful environment where you don't have to worry about being attacked. I want peace, I want them to go back to their villages, but if that doesn't happen, I can work on trying to bring some of them here.

CM: Is there anything else you would like to say on that? Anything on education or anything that is needed in the camp? Any last thoughts?

PK: Well, in terms of the opportunities in class,

the people here need to keep doing the charitable work that we're doing. Especially like you are connecting with girls in Kakuma. That really makes a big difference. It gives them hope, it gives them a chance to think that a better life is possible. In terms of what can be done to change the camp, everything is in the hands of the UN. The UN's mandate is really just to save lives and to protect refugees. The UN is not mandated to give higher education. If we can support initiatives like the World University Service of Canada to make sure that kids who have graduated from high school have the chance to continue their educational dreams, that would be great, but I also know that there is only so much we can do. People here in Canada have families to look after, they have their bills to cover, so charity can only do so much. Where I work, Morneau Shepell, they have done an incredible job of supporting the Morneau Shepell Secondary School for Girls. It's really a good opportunity, but I cannot expect every Canadian to do that, or every other person to do that. We can make small differences. Like you talking to those girls— it really inspires them in a way. You may not know to what extent, but I know for sure that for them to connect and talk to you, and see that people are concerned about them and thinking about them, makes such a big difference. So whatever little effort every inspired Canadian can do to think about the refugees, not necessarily just in Kakuma—if you look in the news today we talk about refugees in Syria, and we don't know what other countries will be affected in the future—so it's just about keeping those who are less fortunate in our thoughts and being thankful for what we have here. I think that's all we can do. There is no one single solution to the situation for all refugees. It's just all charitable people, all people that are concerned, especially young people like yourself who are motivated to not only succeed in your own life, but also to help others your age in faraway countries, that is incredible. And if there is any way I can help bring the stories of those people to life or even talk on their behalf, I would be able to support that.

CM: Your part in the book is actually really important. It's a section of the book hopefully that will be about hope, because for these girls, and for all the kids living in Kakuma, you are hope. They look at you and think that they might be you and if they work that hard, they can be like you.
PK: I know, but I still consider myself as having not achieved much. For them to be able to come to Canada, they could be like me, they could qualify for the scholarship. What difference it makes in people's life is a work in progress. I still consider my life a work in progress, and if I have inspired one or two girls, that is incredible, but I don't see myself as a role model, as someone they can look to. I know that this country has given me an opportunity and I am taking advantage of every bit of it.

From Kakuma to Toronto: Interview with Elizabeth Agutu

Patricia Boychuk

PB: Elizabeth fled South Sudan as a young child to the Kakuma Refugee Camp in Kenya, where she was raised and educated. Elizabeth continued her journey onwards to Canada; she recently did her four-year degree in political economy at Brock University in St. Catherine's, Ontario.

EA: My name is Elizabeth Agutu. I am one of the lucky girls to make it to Canada through the help of people. My life has always been determined by forces of nature that I had no control over. I left South Sudan when I was a year old, or a couple of months old, with my mom—my dad was not there—to Etang Refugee Camp in Ethiopia. I stayed there in the camp not by choice but I was forced to live there because of the circumstances of the war in South Sudan. We lived in Ethiopia for like three or four years and we were forced to leave the camp again when the war broke out in Ethiopia. We left and came to Kakuma. It was a hard journey but we made it. Again, my dad was separated from us and I was with my mom and my other siblings, but then I had three other siblings, so we were four. We came to Kakuma Refugee Camp, where I spent seventeen years of my life as a refugee and a girl in a refugee camp. Kakuma

was not a place I would want to be given the choice, but due to circumstances I should just appreciate that I was lucky to be there other than being in South Sudan, which was raging with war by then. [When we came to] Kakuma, we were given a tent by the UN. Everybody lived in tents for a couple of months or years before they started building permanent or good houses that could help them stay longer. I stayed in Kakuma for seventeen years as I said before, which made it a home for me, so we built our hut and we stayed there with our extended family. Again, my dad was not in the picture. He was in Sudan.

The reason I'm telling this story is to emphasize how important education is to a girl. In Kakuma Refugee Camp, everybody was given the same opportunities. They built schools, but those schools were not well-equipped. In a class you might find eighty students with only one teacher and this made it very hard for students to have one-on-one contact with the teacher. There were not many books and equipment to help students in their daily learning activities, but we tried. In the camp, education for girls is available but not many girls make it. There are so many circumstances that have affected the girls' population in the school. You might find sixty students in a class, and of those there are only ten girls. Girls in Kakuma are discriminated against and are not pushed forward. There are so many things that a girl shall do in the camp that a boy does not do. I did daily home activities, which did not give me time to study for myself and to concentrate in school. I helped at home and cooked, so I didn't have much time for myself, which my brothers had. They had time to go and play with other kids, go and study with their friends, whereas I was forced to stay at home and help people in the kitchen, fetch water, and do other activities that are assumed to be girl jobs and activities in the camp and in African culture. In the camp, these circumstances kind of kill girls' motivation or activity. If you are forced to repeat class three times because you did not pass, you will drop out of school. Girls do not have the security that is needed. They get pregnant when they don't do well in school and they get frustrated since at home they do not get that harmony so they think that getting married will be the simple way out of this. This has forced many girls to drop out of school and not do well in the camp.

I was lucky because I had a family that had a little bit of education and background that knew what education means to anybody, whether you are a girl or a boy, and I was lucky that my dad in Sudan was supportive by sending us a little. I was taken to boarding school in grade four, where my brothers and I went to the same school, which is an opportunity most of my other extended family or other girls in Kakuma did not get. When I was taken to boarding school, this helped me to concentrate on my

studies and I did better or best compared to even other boys. I was lucky to get a scholarship to high school after my primary school, which many girls would not have gotten, because in the camp they couldn't get the grades I did. It's not that I'm better—I know any other girl is the same with me. I also worked hard in secondary school, where I was sponsored by GRS (Global Rescue Services), an NGO that helps refugee students to get a better chance to get out of the camp through school. I passed my high school and again, I was lucky to get a scholarship from WUSC, which brought me to Canada. Here in Canada, this is my fourth year, and I still always have in my heart that if there is a way to help any other girl, I will do it. They could be here with me, they could get that opportunity that I got.

PB: If you hadn't received your scholarships for secondary education and post-secondary that brought you to Canada where would you be today without your education?
EA: In the camp, when you don't get this opportunity, your life ends, there's no way out. You are a refugee, you can't go back to South Sudan, and if you go back to South Sudan what will you do with a primary education? You wouldn't be able to help yourself or even society. Given this opportunity, I have achieved my dreams, but if I was back there, I would be married now with a couple of kids, maybe five, because my mom got married at the age of fifteen.

PB: I imagine that your life has changed dramatically since you've arrived in Canada in respect to culture, the economy, even the climate and university life at Brock.

What opportunities are on the horizon for you once you graduate, which should be coming up shortly?

EA: I'm excited but again, I'm scared. There are so many opportunities. I went to school here and in Africa you don't go to a university or even a college. The majority of students in those classes are boys, not girls. When I came to Brock, the number of girl students was more than boy students, which is amazing. Here women are given opportunity and they can be grateful for that. I'll be done with my school and I've always wanted to give back to society. I wanted to take political sciences and economy because I think that my life was determined by these forces, political wars or economy, which cause people to care less about normal citizens, and I think that is why my life has been about this. I want to work and give back to society, either by working with NGOs or the UN, just to give back and appreciate how other people changed my life. My life has been determined by the help of other good people outside of here

PB: Will you go back to Kakuma to work if the opportunity presents itself?

EA: I would love to give back to my people— I call them my people, even though they are people from different countries, as they make up the camp. That has forced me to appreciate and live with other people and to share. I would love to share what I've gained and give it back to people who really need it.

PB: Along your journey, did you ever struggle or lose sight of your dream?

EA: Yes, I think I struggled after my high school.

I never knew that I would get an opportunity to come here or even to go to further education. I never knew that I would maybe go to university and be somebody else. I thought my life would just end with my high school education, but along the way, I thought that I could make it if other people can make it. There were scholarships, so I looked for how to apply.

PB: What would make the greatest difference in the life of a young girl in Kakuma as she begins her journey as you did?

EA: Education. I'm here in Canada where education is freely available and people don't take advantage of that and it has made me really appreciate being given this opportunity. Education will change the lives of girls in the camp, pushing them and giving them every resource they need. This will really change their life as I believe it has changed mine. I am the living proof of this, of the chance that I was given. So I believe, given every resource—being taken to boarding school, being given enough resources from the teachers—their life and their journey will be one that is good to them and to society at large.

PB: If you had one last message that you would like to leave us with today, what would that be?

EA: I will say that a woman starts with a girl and a girl is the future of every country, regardless of where they are from. They have the power to bring an immediate change that we can feel. If you have a chance to help any other girl out there, please do. I would give anything for my voice to help these girls. I would be so thankful for that.

Reflection

Reflection
Clare Morneau

I feel privileged to have the chance to talk to these Kakuma girls and learn about their lives. I'm honoured they were willing to share their stories with me, my fellow students at Havergal College, and with you.

I have learned so much in the process of making this book. Christine, Sarah, Lula, Nhial, Nyimuch, Fardosa, Rita, Zahira, Amach, and Esther have taught me about the world, about refugees, and most importantly, about the value of education. I used to take my education for granted, not knowing how lucky I am to attend a top-ranked high school and have the chance to attend university if I so choose. Meeting girls like Lula has inspired me and opened my eyes—this girl my age has only known life as a refugee. She wants so badly to be a citizen, to study to be a doctor, and to contribute to her family and country of origin, Somalia.

These Kakuma girls are fighting for their education and will do anything to go to university. They are working hard, dreaming of becoming doctors, pilots, or journalists and improving their and their family's lives. Why shouldn't they have the opportunities I and other Canadian girls have? I am inspired to take advantage of every opportunity I am lucky enough to have, and I am motivated to help these refugee girls get the university education they deserve.

Girls' education is a fundamental part of success in countries around the world. Every single one of the girls featured in this book, along with many of their friends in Kakuma, will undoubtedly change the world.

Their determination, strength, and resilience is amazing, yet all girls in Kakuma and other camps and conflict zones need their rights respected. This also takes determination and the commitment of families and communities, and at the highest level, political will and funding from political leaders and educators.

I'm grateful my friends, classmates, and teachers also wanted to meet these Kakuma girls and open their hearts and lives to them through a letter-writing exchange.

The world is a bigger place for me now. It's scarier knowing about so many horrific realities for girls in conflict zones and flight, but it's also a more beautiful place knowing all these girls.

And at the same time, the world's a bit smaller. I recently met an Ethiopian man, a newcomer to Toronto, and I was excited that I knew something more about his country. Through Nyimuch, who also fled from Ethiopia, I knew more about the conflict and drought this man had fled. His presence adds a new voice to Canada's story. This book made me think a lot about all that makes a community: schools, hospitals, tranquility. As my Canadian friend Alie says, home is not a physical place but a place where people give and receive love, and as Zahira from Sudan shares, home is a place of origin but also a place to live in peace and harmony.

I bring up the refugee crisis in many conversations I have, hoping to encourage others to get involved and support education for refugees. I am quick to challenge anyone who believes refugees should not be accepted into Canada, because I believe every refugee deserves a chance at a better life. I hope this book sheds more light on life in a refugee camp, because I think it is little known. I have no doubt that every movement these refugee girls take towards rebuilding their countries or shaping new countries if they are resettled, will be one in the right direction—one that leads to a more stable, equal world, where refugees are treated like humans and no longer have to experience situations where they spend a great portion of their lives as refugees.

These girls have affected my life in a way that I would not have ever imagined possible. They have changed my priorities, my conversations, and my ideas about education and the world. I hope you and other readers who meet these girls are affected by their stories and do something to help, to raise awareness, to write a letter to a girl in Kakuma, to support girls' education, be it in Kakuma or anywhere. If every person knows more about these refugee camps, and understands that living in each and every refugee camp is extremely difficult, there could be so much more empathy for refugees, and much more support.

I believe that if we support girls we will support the world.

Left to right: Nancy McCain, Adut Dau, Lula Abdulkhadir Modhar, Esther Nyakong,
Clare Morneau, Irene Kinyanjui, Christine Bachoke, Sarah Nyajuok Gik.

Afterword

In February 2016, I travelled to Kenya and was lucky enough to meet several of the girls who are profiled in this book. I was supposed to travel into Kakuma Refugee Camp and visit the Morneau Shepell Secondary School for Girls, but there was an unexpected terrorist threat from Al-Shabaab against the camp. This threat was against Westerners and the UN, so I unfortunately could not go. Not only was it disappointing that I could not visit the camp, but this is frightening because it suggests that Kakuma may be getting more dangerous.

Then a beautiful thing happened: the UNHCR decided to bring five of the Morneau Shepell Secondary School students to Nairobi to meet me, four of whom shared their personal stories in this book. Christine walked into the UNHCR Kenya headquarters first and pretty much tackled me with a hug. It was almost like déjà vu— I already knew so much about these girls that it felt like I had known them for years. I don't think I've ever smiled that much before. I really feel like I have a connection to Kakuma. These girls inspire me every day and I think that they will inspire so many other people as long as their stories are told and their voices are heard.

It's very easy to forget about the need for girls' education in many parts of the world when you're living in a society that accepts and promotes it. It's much harder when you meet girls who are extremely promising, but fear that they will not be able to continue their education. You can't ignore the desire and need for secondary and university education when you meet these refugee girls face to face. When you hear Lula talk about how she wants to be a neurosurgeon and see her excitement over a science book, the only thing you can think about is how to get her to university. When Christine shows you a short video about girls' education that she helped write and direct, her desire to educate the rest of the world about Kakuma is obvious. When Esther talks about her older sister's missed chance at a university education and the lack of hope in the camp, you realize how incredibly difficult it is to survive in Kakuma. Every one of these girls is a fighter. They are fighting for their families, for their education, and for their right to be recognized as people.

Before we left, they all hastily wrote down their Facebook information for me, making me promise that I would message them as soon as I landed in Canada, and Christine handed me a short letter to give to her partner Stephanie at Havergal. It was sad to leave, but as someone taught me, in Nairobi, we don't say goodbye, we say see you soon.

Kakuma girls are unforgettable. Their stories, their promise, their incredible perseverance and personal strength is astounding. With a university education, girls like Christine, Sarah, Esther, Lula, and Adut will not just be unforgettable to me, but they'll be unforgettable to the world. I can't wait to see where they go— because I know they're going places.

Acknowledgements

This book is a collection of voices, and would not have been possible without incredible support and input from many people.

On the Kakuma side, my thanks to the UNHCR, particularly Fortunata Ngonyani, Mohamed Hure, and Cathy Wachiaya, who have fostered and encouraged the relationship between the girls in Kakuma and Canada. Thanks to Joy Wafula, Raphael Sungu, Joel Ndingi, John Ekamais, Sarah Pinky, Edward Olang, and Sabela Muthoni for supporting girls' education, all students and new arrivals in Kakuma Refugee Camp.

At Havergal, thanks to Ms. Pink, Ms. Rowe, and the Forum for Change. They are all incredibly supportive of this project, and understand how important it is to me.

I am particularly grateful to my book team, who went above and beyond in everything they did for the book. Thanks to Jjumba Martin, Doug Laxdal, Isabel Foo, Laura Legge and Pamela Martin. Thanks also to Sarah Cha for helping me research and learn more about the refugee crisis and Kakuma. I also need to thank Morneau Shepell for everything they have done to support the girls living in Kakuma Refugee Camp and for allowing me to be a part of it. I extend my thanks to Panther Kuol and Elizabeth Agutu, who were willing to share their stories with me and the world. They are sources of inspiration for not only refugees but for me and my friends.

I also need to thank my family for their endless love and support. They have been so excited throughout this whole process.

Most importantly, I need to thank all of the girls involved in the partnership and the book. The girls in Toronto have shared their thoughts and their letters, and have been incredibly enthusiastic in getting to know refugee girls on the other side of the world. It is inspiring to see them so excited. The girls in Kakuma Refugee Camp have shared their hopes and their dreams. I am so thankful that they told me their stories— their words are inspirational and moving.

Lastly, thank you to Carol Devine, my editor. She has stood by me every step of this journey. Without her constant cheerfulness, resourcefulness, and guidance, this book would not have been possible. Carol, you truly were a blessing.

And thank you to everyone who picks up a copy of this book. You are supporting the education of refugee girls and making dreams come true.

Get Involved

HOW TO GET INVOLVED

As you can probably tell, I believe that educating refugee girls is extremely important. After reading this book, I hope that you understand why so many refugee girls deserve the education they are so desperate to receive. If you feel at all inclined to help these girls reach their dreams of attending university, please do not hesitate! All of the proceeds from this book and any donations received will go towards setting up university scholarships for refugee girls at the Morneau Shepell Secondary School for Girls.

Donate

Any funds donated through this website will go towards sending a girl attending the Morneau Shepell Secondary School for Girls to university. To donate, please see www.kakumagirls.org.

If you would like, it is also possible to donate to any of the organizations mentioned in the 'Who to Know' section. All of these organizations use donations to help refugees living in Kakuma Refugee Camp, along with other places, and would welcome any help that you can provide.

Write

If you are a student and would like to write to girls at Morneau Shepell Secondary School for Girls please send a letter to the address below. They would love to hear from other students around the world.

Morneau Shepell Secondary School For Girls
c/o UNHCR Representation in Kenya
P.O. Box 43801-00100, Nairobi, Kenya

Ask

If you have any questions, please do not hesitate to access our website at www.kakumagirls.org or email me at info@kakumagirls.org.

WHO TO KNOW
UNHCR
The Office of the United Nations High Commissioner for Refugees is mandated to lead and co-ordinate international action to protect refugees and resolve refugee problems worldwide. Its primary purpose is to safeguard the rights and well-being of refugees. The agency strives to ensure that everyone can exercise the right to seek asylum and find safe refuge in another state, with the option to return home voluntarily, integrate locally or resettle in a third country. The UNHCR implements Morneau Shepell Secondary School for Girls.

FilmAid
FilmAid uses the power of film and media to transcend language and literacy, bringing life-saving information, psychological relief and hope to refugees and other communities in need around the globe. FilmAid creates media to inform marginalized populations about their rights, their safety, health and community. It also trains youth in modern communications so they can advocate for their own rights and their community's needs. In Kakuma, FilmAid screens thematic films preceded by messages on public health or cultural practices that affect girls' education. For example, for the Somali and Turkana communities, films address early marriage. The filmmakers do a pre-screening survey on perceptions and then survey again after the film to find out if and how viewer's perceptions may have changed.

Windle Trust Kenya
Windle Trust helps implement Morneau Shepell Secondary School for Girls. It's a non-governmental organization in Kenya and a member of Windle Trust International Federation. The Trust started in 1977 to assist refugees and Kenyans in need. It focuses on educational scholarships for students in the camp and the host community and works towards building girl-friendly school environments, providing targeted support to female learners, and generating parent and community support for girls' education.

Malala Fund
Inspired by co-founders Malala and Ziauddin Yousafzai, Malala Fund's goal is to enable girls to complete 12 years of safe, quality education so that they can achieve their potential and be positive change-makers in their families and communities. The Fund works with partners all over the world helping to empower girls and amplify their voices. They invest in local education leaders and programmes; and advocate for more resources for education and safe schools for every child.

FURTHER READING
· Malala Yousafzai, *I am Malala: The Girl Who Stood Up for Education and Was Shot by the Taliban*

· Dave Eggars, *What is the What: The Autobiography of Valentino Achak Deng*

Chronology
UNHCR, Refugee Crises, and Women and Girls

20 August 1921: the Council of the League of Nations appointed Dr. Fridtjof Nansen as the High Commissioner for Refugees.

30 September 1930: The International Nansen Office for Refugees was created by League of Nations Resolution, specifying that its work was to be concluded by December 31, 1938. From mid-World War II through 1946, European refugee issues were addressed by the United Nations Relief and Rehabilitation Agency (UNRRA). The International Refugee Organization (IRO) operated between 1946 and 1951.

December 14, 1950: UNHCR emerged in the wake of World War II to help Europeans displaced by that conflict. The Office of the United Nations High Commissioner for Refugees was established by the United Nations General Assembly with a three-year mandate to complete its work and then disband. The following year the United Nations Convention relating to the Status of Refugees—the legal foundation for helping refugees and the basic statute guiding UNHCR's work— was adopted.

1 January 1951: UNHCR was established by the United Nations General Assembly.

1954: UNHCR won the Nobel Peace Prize for its groundbreaking work in helping the refugees of Europe.

1956: UNHCR faced its first major emergency—the outpouring of refugees when Soviet forces crushed the Hungarian Revolution.

1960s: The decolonization of Africa produced the first of that continent's numerous refugee crises requiring UNHCR intervention in the sixties. The UNHCR responded to displacement crises in Asia and Latin America in the next decade.

1979: The Soviet Union occupied Afghanistan, sending as many as five million people fleeing.

1981: More than a quarter century after winning a Nobel Peace Prize, UNHCR again received the award for what had become worldwide assistance to refugees, with the citation noting the political obstacles facing the organization.

1984: Ethiopians first sought refuge in Kenya in 1984 when a massive famine hit the country. Then in 1991 a new large group arrived when Colonel Mengitsu's government was overthrown by the Ethiopian People's Revolutionary Democratic Front.

1985: The first working group on refugee women was convened to advocate for the needs of women affected by conflict. The working group's lobbying activities resulted in the 1989 appointment of a Senior Coordinator for Refugee Women to UNHCR.

1990: UNHCR adopted the first-ever policy on refugee women's protection. The guidelines explicitly acknowledged exposure to sexual violence as a vulnerability of refugee women and called upon the humanitarian community to address it within its protection mandate.

1992–1995: New waves of refugees flee to Europe from the Balkan wars.

1994: Rwandan Genocide—up to a million Tutsi and moderate Hutus were killed during an orchestrated crime of humanity.

1994–1997 The Great Lakes Crisis in Africa. This refers to the political and refugee crisis and violence that gripped the Great Lakes region starting with the Rwandan genocide. In late April 1994 there was a massive and rapid refugee exodus to neighbouring countries including Zaire (now Democratic Republic of Congo) and Tanzania.

1995: UNHCR published *Sexual Violence Against Refugees: Guidelines on Protection and Response,* which highlighted some of the major legal, medical and psychosocial components of prevention of, and response to, sexual violence.

2000: At the start of the 21st century UNHCR helped with major refugee crises in Africa, such as the Democratic Republic of the Congo and Somalia, and Asia, especially the thirty-year-old Afghan refugee situation. UNHCR had been asked to use its expertise to help many people who had been internally displaced by conflict. Less visibly, it had expanded its role in helping stateless people, a largely overlooked group numbering millions of people in danger of being denied basic rights because they do not have any citizenship. In some parts of the world, such as Africa and Latin America, the original 1951 mandate was strengthened by agreement on regional legal instruments.

2000: UN Security Council Resolution (SCR) 1325 on Women, Peace and Security was adopted. It was the first SCR to link women to the peace and security agenda. It recognized that women are disproportionately affected by conflict and calls for their active participation at all levels of decision-making in conflict prevention, conflict resolution, peace processes, post-conflict peacebuilding, and governance.

2002: The international media broke the story of sexual exploitation and abuse committed by humanitarian staff against refugee women and girls in West Africa. The public outrage and embarrassment led to an increase in attention and funds for gender-based violence interventions.

2003: The UN General Assembly extended the organization's mandate "until the refugee problem is solved." In Darfur there were more than 2.6 million internally displaced people and more than 250,000 Darfurians living in refugee camps in Chad. The Iraq war started in 2003, displacing a large number of Iraqis, largely into neighbouring countries.

2008–2013: The UN Security Council adopted four resolutions framing conflict-related sexual violence as a threat to international peace and security: 1820 (2008), 1888 (2009), 1960 (2010), and 2106 (2013). This included the appointment of a Special Representative to the Secretary General on Sexual Violence in Armed Conflict.

2011: When protests in Syria degenerated into a civil war stalemate, the largest chapter of refugee movement in history began.

2015: Over 9 million Syrians fled their homes since 2011. By mid-2015 4 million had fled to Syria's neighbours Turkey, Lebanon, Jordan, and Iraq. Within Syria, over 7.6 million had been been internally displaced. Meanwhile, less than 150,000 Syrians declared asylum in the European Union. Women and girls comprised the majority of Syrians fleeing. They report harassment, violence, isolation and chronic poverty. The UN reports a worrying increase in Syrian child brides in Jordan.

2015: Unprecedented migration to Europe of Syrian, Eritrean, Afghan, West African, and other refugees and migrants. Refugees often met closed borders, or faced treacherous sea routes. The UNHCR appealed to concerned national authorities in Europe to take measures to ensure the protection of women and girls, including through providing adequate and safe reception facilities. Refugees in Europe represented less than 10 per cent of the number of people in flight globally in 2015. The UNHCR warns of a looming refugee crisis in Central America where like elsewhere, girls and women are especially vulnerable to abuse in mass displacement.

2016: High Commissioner for Refugees, Mr. Filippo Grandi urged governments to invest more energy and resources to solving wars and conflicts and provide solutions to the causes of refugee crises. Refugees need resettlement, humanitarian visas and family reunification. They need safe and legal pathways. Host countries with vast numbers of refugees like Lebanon and Kenya need better support.

Glossary

Regardless of people's legal status they need to be treated humanely and with dignity

Asylum Seekers: People who are seeking international protection. An asylum seeker is someone whose claim has not yet been finally decided by UNHCR or authorities of the country in which he or she has requested refugee status. Not every asylum seeker will ultimately be recognized as a refugee, but every refugee is initially an asylum seeker.

Dadaab: Dadaab is in Garissa County, Kenya, near Somalia's border. UNHCR, which manages the Dadaab complex, set up the first camps there in 1991. This followed a civil war in Somalia that had culminated in the fall of Mogadishu and overthrow of the central government in 1991. Like Kakuma, Dadaab is over capacity and suffers from a lack of resources. Dadaab hosts the largest refugee camp in the world, with over 329,000 residents in 2015.

Durable Solution: UNHCR's primary purpose is to safeguard the rights and well-being of refugees, with an ultimate goal to help find durable solutions that will allow refugees to rebuild their lives in dignity and peace. There are three solutions open to refugees where the UNHCR can help: voluntary repatriation; local integration; or resettlement to a third country in situations where it is impossible for a person to go back home or remain in the host country.

Forced Migration: The International Association for the Study of Forced Migration (IASFM) describes it as "the movements of refugees and internally displaced people displaced by conflict as well as people displaced by natural or environmental disasters, chemical or nuclear disasters, famine, or development projects."

Gender-Based Violence (GBV): This refers to violence that targets individuals or groups on the basis of their gender. The UN Office of the High Commissioner for Human Rights Committee on the Elimination of Discrimination against Women defines it as "violence that is directed against a woman because she is a woman or that affects women disproportionately." This includes acts that inflict physical, mental, or sexual harm or suffering, the threat of such acts, coercion, and other deprivations of liberty. Boys and men can also be victims of gender-based violence.

Havergal College: A private girls' school in Toronto, Canada.

Internally Displaced People (IDPs): People who are forcibly displaced within their countries of origin or habitual residence but who have not crossed an internationally recognized state border. People may be internally displaced as a result of armed conflicts, situations of generalized violence, violations of human rights, or natural or human-made disasters.

International Organization of Migration (IOM): Established in 1951, IOM is the principal intergovernmental organization in the field of migration. IOM works to help ensure the orderly and humane management of migration, to promote international cooperation on migration issues, to assist in the search for practical solutions to migration problems, and to provide humanitarian assistance to migrants in need, whether they are refugees, displaced persons, or other uprooted people.

International Rescue Committee (IRC): Responds to the world's worst humanitarian crises and helps people to survive and rebuild their lives. IRC teams provide health care, infrastructure development, education, and economic support to people in more than forty countries, with special programs designed for women and children.

Kakuma: A town in Turkana County, in the northwestern region of Kenya that has been the site of Kakuma Refugee Camp since 1991. Most refugees are from nearby South Sudan and Somalia.

Lagga: A dry riverbed that runs through Kakuma Refugee Camp. Several girls say it's an unsafe place for girls to go because of the risk of sexual violation.

Lost Boys/Lost Girls: The Lost Boys and Girls of Sudan are a large group of people who were forced to leave their homes as unaccompanied children following regional strife between North and South Sudan in the late 1980s. In late 1991, the first lot of Lost Boys arrived in Kakuma Refugee Camp. Thousands more arrived in 1992.

Lutheran World Federation (LWF): A Christian organization representing over 72 million Christians in 98 countries dedicated to serving those in need and advocating for a more just, peaceful, and reconciled world. It supports the Reception Centre in Kakuma.

Migrant: Migrants choose to move not because of a direct threat of persecution or death, but mainly to improve their lives by finding work, or to receive an education, reunite with their family, or other reasons. Unlike refugees who cannot safely return home, migrants face no such impediment to return.

Morneau Shepell: Canada's largest human resource firm and supporter of the Morneau Shepell Secondary School for Girls.

Morneau Shepell Secondary School for Girls: A girls' boarding school in Kakuma Refugee Camp, Kenya.

Polygamous Marriage: The practice of one husband having two or more concurrent wives (polygyny), is legal in over fifty countries. To ensure women's rights, activists advocate for the abolition of the practice.

Protracted Refugee Situation: When refugees find themselves in a long-lasting and intractable state of limbo. Their lives may not be at risk, but their basic rights and essential economic, social, and psychological needs remain unfulfilled after years in exile. A refugee in this situation is often unable to break free from reliance on external assistance.

Refoulement: The forcible return of refugees or asylum-seekers to a country where they are liable to be subjected to persecution.

Refugee: Legally defined as someone fleeing his or her country of origin due to fear of persecution for reasons of race, nationality, religion, or association with a particular social or political group and opinion.

Resettlement: The transfer of refugees from an asylum country to another state that has agreed to admit them and ultimately grant them permanent settlement. UNHCR is mandated by its Statute and the UN General Assembly Resolutions to undertake resettlement as one of the three durable solutions. Resettlement is unique in that it is the only durable solution that involves the relocation of refugees from an asylum country to a third country. Of the 14.4 million refugees of concern to UNHCR around the world, fewer than one per cent are submitted for resettlement.

Returnees: Refugees who choose voluntarily to return to their country of origin. In some circumstances, their return is assisted by the UNHCR and they receive support after they arrive.

Stateless Persons: People who are not recognized by any country as citizens and who consequently lack the protections flowing from citizenship. Article 1 of the 1954 Convention relating to the Status of Stateless Persons sets out the criteria for statelessness in international law.

United Nations High Commissioner for Refugees (UNHCR): The Office of the United Nations High Commissioner for Refugees was established on December 14, 1950 by the United Nations General Assembly. The agency is mandated to lead and coordinate international action to protect refugees and resolve refugee problems worldwide. Oversees Morneau Shepell Secondary School for Girls.

UN Convention on Refugees: The 1951 Convention relating to the Status of Refugees is the key legal document defining who is a refugee, as well as what rights refugees have and the legal obligations of states. The 1967 Protocol removed geographical and temporal restrictions from the Convention.

Warehousing: An increasing number of host states respond to protracted refugee situations by containing refugees in isolated and insecure refugee camps, typically in border regions and far from the governing regimes. Many host governments now require the vast majority of refugees to live in designated camps and place restrictions on those seeking to leave the camps for employment or education. This trend, recently termed the 'warehousing' of refugees, has significant human rights and economic implications.

World Food Programme (WFP): Created in 1961, The World Food Programme is the world's largest humanitarian agency fighting hunger worldwide.

Windle Trust Kenya (WT): A non-governmental organization in Kenya and a member of Windle Trust International Federation. WT Kenya was started in 1977 to assist refugees and Kenyans in need. It focuses on educational scholarships for students in the camp and in the host community and helps run Morneau Shepell Secondary School for Girls in Kakuma.

World University Service of Canada (WUSC): A leading Canadian non-profit organization in international development, committed to building a more equitable and sustainable world. WUSC supports international development projects worldwide and education activities in Canadian universities, including for refugee students.

Sources

"BBC Country Profiles." *BBC.* news.bbc.co.uk/2/hi/country_ profiles/default.stm

De Montclos, Marc-Antoine P., and Peter M. Kagwanja. "Refugee Camps or Cities? The Socio-Economic Dynamics of the Dadaab and Kakuma Camps in Northern Kenya." *Journal of Refugee Studies* 13, no. 2 (2000): 205–222.

Feyissa Demo, Abebe. "Riding on the back of a tortoise." *Forced Migration Review* 33 (2009).

"Kenya 2015 Country Operations Profile." *UNHCR.* www.unhcr.org/ pages/49e483a16.html

"Kenya Kakuma Operational Update 16–29 February, 2016." *UNHCR.* http://www.unocha.org/aggregator/ sources/69

"Kenya Sub-Office Kakuma Operation Camp Profile, 30 June, 2015" *UNHCR.*

Kristof, Nicholas. "A Rain of Bombs in the Nuba Mountains." *New York Times,* June 20, 2015.

---. "A Toddler's Death in a Foxhole." *New York Times.* July 2, 2015.

Kirui, P., and J., Mwaruvie. "The Dilemma of Hosting Refugees: A Focus on the Insecurity in North-Eastern Kenya." International Journal of Business and Social Science 3, no. 8 (April 2012).

Oka, Rahul. "Coping with the Refugee Wait: The Role of Consumption, Normalcy, and Dignity in Refugee Lives at Kakuma Refugee Camp, Kenya." *American Anthropologist* 116, no. 1 (2014): 23–37.

Otieno, Peter (assisted by Don Owino and Silvano Ndwiga) and Dorothy Gazarwa. *World Food Programme Joint Assessment Mission – Kenya Refugee Operation Dadaab (23–27 June 2014) and Kakuma (30 June–1 July 2014) Refugee camps.* World Food Programme, 2014.

"Solutions needed to stem global refugee crisis, says Grandi." *UNHCR.* 7 January 2016. www.unhcr.org/ 568e82ff6.html

Sperling, Gene B., and Rebecca Winthrop. *What Works in Girls' Education: Evidence for the World's Best Investment.* Washington: Brookings Institute Press, 2015.

Students of Morneau Shepell Secondary School for Girls

Mercy Eyasu Lalle
Mary Ayen Ukech
Fozia Abdirashid
Iqra Yusuf Musa
Rahma Abdikadir
Muna Buton Ali
Malyun Abdi Hakim
Martha John Korok
Mauwa Kalunga
Namoe Lolem Amoo
Leyla Osman
Sofia Toto Bulmwengu
Shamso Mohammed
Khadija Mohammed
Afso Abdulwahid
Nyawal Gatluak
Nyanthie Mayang
Hani Abdi Awil
Ifrah Yasin
Kadra Ahmed
Claire Lotenea Longor
Hawa Abdi Aziz Abdi
Zamzamali Noor
Saado Ali Noor
Cheramba Jepkoech Ann
Aliet Bior Alier
Lodei Anjelina Nabuin
Sadiyo Osman Ahamed
Santina Iliha Mauro
Pauline Nakorok Kobongin
Fortune Zandizo Nyagahama
Mandek Salim Mohamed
Nawal Msutafa Aabi
Hayat Adem Mahamoud
Khadija Aden Hussein
Susan Nyanchiek Jacob
Nyabol Ngor Kuol
Sunday Ibalu Achila
Ariela Irakoze
Ikonga Achuto Leita
Maryan Mohammed Hassan

Ali Mary Ayen
Atong M Rhoda
Nyaluk Kuol Deng
Deng Gak Jeniffer
Nasibo Osman Guyo
Zamzam Hassan Adey
Kifah Abdi Halane
Esther John Ambadi
Flora Sida Aziz
Hayat Ismail Adam
Aluko Abakar Daldum
Farhiya Mohamed
Maryan Mohammed
Fowsiyo Hassan Abdulle
Habibu Abdi
Sirat Abdi Mohamed
Urshalim Zacaria Al-Muraka
Ebenyo Jully Akamais
Ingis Aden Mohamed
Dorcas Ebei Lokidor
Moruese Lokol Judy
Muwada Ali Abdalla
Priscilla Peter Anur
Anadi Hessin Mahammud
Esinyon Joy Akidor
Riba Kamal Ali
Martha Nakiru Natemo
Ikran Abdi Adullahi
Nada Sedik Hamed
Nabanda David
Harriet Ropan Jodi
Malembe Byamungu
Marieangel Ushindi Khashindi
Said Rukia Musa
Akai Jacinta
Gloria David Leila
Yolanda Salumu Busanga
Obisitu Teshome Hika
Amer Akech Akook
Leila Galgalo Guyo
Elizabeth Nyibul Kolnyin

Yom Madol Anyang
Monica Atueny Deng
Nyalit Choul Yok
Kuchi Kuku Chururu
Nasira Luka Abdalla
Sirra Jally Hassan
Umutoni Lygie
Mayen Atem Nyacueth
Mark Magdaline
Angeline Gatkol
Chikosa Malau Lugazo
Jamila Dadiri
Adut Dau Deng
Achol Maniem Maluak
Mukasa Irene Mariam
Sharizat James Komi
Grace Nanjala
Hellen Nakeny
Abdihakim Saharo
Mary Adheu Akuilen
Salima Gabriel
Rausa Luke Ras
Esther Nyakong Bethow
Asma Maki Hussein
Uwemana Maria
Naiboi Martha
Fausia Abirisak Yusuf
Abdi Samira Botan
Nyonkuru Uwera Harriet
Fardosa Ali Hassan
Chali Peter Lominat
Arkanjelo Atee Flora
Idwa Martin Elia
Amina Abdulkhadir
Peter Nyesery Gony
Eng'or Jacinta Naukot
Laurhyn Akal Lomanat
Habiba Ibrahim Musa
Ibtisam Haji Madi
Atabo Rachel Kainza
Ekaale Caroline

Ruthrosy Emmanah
Maximillan Akori
Elam Ali Kuku
Lopie Sylvia Ewoton
Sarah Ikamat Maide
Angelina Nyadek
Zakia John Idriss Tutu
Veronicah Epungure
Maryama Abdikadir Mohamed
Nyibuk Dak Khong
Lomoe Magdaline
Sharon Napungure
Nhial Alek Tabitha
Nyanchop Monychol
Abuk Chuol
Rita Monday Tom
Angeth Atem
Abalo Charles Concy
Nancy Langoya
Sarah Wani
Amal Mark Concy
Joyce Sunday
Angelina Mawia
Majdi Kodi
Zinap Yusup
Kelu Ibrahim
Munira Ibrahim
Martha Nabii
Hawaya Mohammed
Muridi Magene
Chaangwa Abdirahaman
Namoi Elizabeth
Hawa Ooman
Nyadeng Deng
Hawa Yusuf
Anjelo Akob
Brenda Mzee
Asha Saleh Hassan
Samara Hussein
Kisma Ismail
Nadio Etoot
Terry Awesti
Mayuat Wuor Angeer
Marina Nyamude
Achol Awan Mabior
Lawrence Nakang

Elga Nakiru
Maryam Abdulaziz
Fatuma Noor Mohamed
Banza Marie
Tiengthon Rebecca
Nyalinglat Paljak
Divine Benediction
Achol Dong Anguei
Ngimoe Centrine Akai
Latek Abonyo Lajabu
Libin Abdinasir Dean
Ayen Malual Kur
Nyimuch Chuol Wel
Nyanga Catherine
Anyango Okeny
Suleiman Nura
Rebbecca Akur
Albino Akongo
Lozenge Ebby
Faiso Mohamed
Nania Omar
Raila Alamin
Hakim Nawala
Bashir Koshe Lalo
Oheny Ifere
Rhoda Daniel
Alek Dut
Nancy Hamed
Gladys Elim
Inham Mousin
Kachiri Osman
Widad Ibrahim
Rooo Ihuro
Dhieu Youl Anyier
Sarah Kashare
Nanjala Priscilla
Laura Zachary
Mami Idriss
Gamar Ayoub
Musangania Kanyere
Nakiru Atuol
Monical Nabai
Lula Abdulkhadir Modhar
Alimlim Eloiloi
Iman Abdirahman
Sarah Nyajuok Gik

Rukia Yusuf
Salima Saleh
Zahira Habila Ariss
Otieno Anchieng
Esther Kulang
Gatkuoth Deng
Idiong Lodulo
Kamuka Ismail
Majida M Angola
Aza Omar Musa
Nassirin Hassan
Anige Ashim
Leyla Noor
Konyo Musa
Veronica Kodi
Magadam J Tutu
Shukuru Bachoke
Toto Almarin
Susan Kunda
Josepk Nakeny
Ahmed Sowodo
Khadjo Ahmed
Adhieu Tabitha
Imoya T Joyce
Rose Ekitela
Mary Moses
Joyce John
Arsity Shamsudin
Susan Komi
Anige Omar
Nyajouk Lual
Amach Mabior
Iklao Samir
Manal Simon Kodi